Daily Science

GRADE 3

Writing: Barbara Allman
Content Editing: Marilyn Evans
Barbara Price
James Spears
Andrea Weiss
Copy Editing: Cathy Harber
Laurie Westrich
Art Direction: Cheryl Puckett
Illustration: Ruth Flanigan
Design/Production: Susan Bigger
Kathy Kopp

EMC 5013

Evan-Moor®
Helping Children Learn

Visit
teaching-standards.com
to view a correlation
of this book.
This is a free service.

**Correlated to
Current Standards**

**Congratulations on your purchase of some of the
finest teaching materials in the world.**

*Photocopying the pages in this book
is permitted for <u>single-classroom use only</u>.
Making photocopies for additional classes
or schools is prohibited.*

For information about other Evan-Moor products, call 1-800-777-4362,
fax 1-800-777-4332, or visit our website, www.evan-moor.com.
Entire contents © 2009 EVAN-MOOR CORP.
18 Lower Ragsdale Drive, Monterey, CA 93940-5746. Printed in USA.

CPSIA: Bang Printing, 600 West Technology Drive, Palmdale, CA 93551 [7/2019]

Contents

What's in This Book?

Daily Science provides daily activity pages grouped into six units, called Big Ideas, that explore a wide range of topics based on the national standards for life, earth, and physical sciences. Every Big Idea includes five weekly lessons. The first four weeks each center around an engaging question that taps into students' natural curiosity about the world to develop essential concepts and content vocabulary. The fifth week of each unit offers a hands-on activity and review pages for assessment and extra practice.

The short 10- to 15-minute activities in *Daily Science* allow you to supplement your science instruction every day while developing reading comprehension and practicing content vocabulary.

Unit Introduction

Key science concepts and national science standards covered in the unit are indicated.

Background information is provided on the topic, giving you the knowledge you need to present the unit concepts confidently.

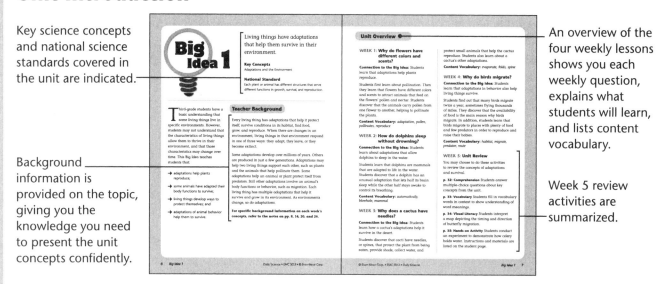

An overview of the four weekly lessons shows you each weekly question, explains what students will learn, and lists content vocabulary.

Week 5 review activities are summarized.

Weekly Lessons (Weeks 1–4)

Each week begins with a teacher page that provides additional background information specific to the weekly question.

Ideas are given for presenting the daily activity pages, including content vocabulary and materials needed for any demonstrations or group activities.

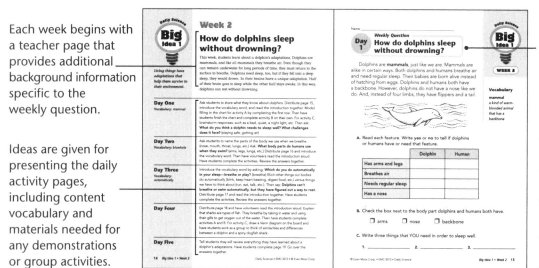

The student activity pages for Days 1–4 of each week use an inquiry-based model to help students answer the weekly question and understand fundamental concepts related to the Big Idea.

You may wish to have students complete the pages independently or collaboratively.

Weekly Lessons, continued

Each student page begins with a short introduction. —

Activities include a variety of writing, comprehension, vocabulary, critical thinking, visual literacy, and oral language practice.

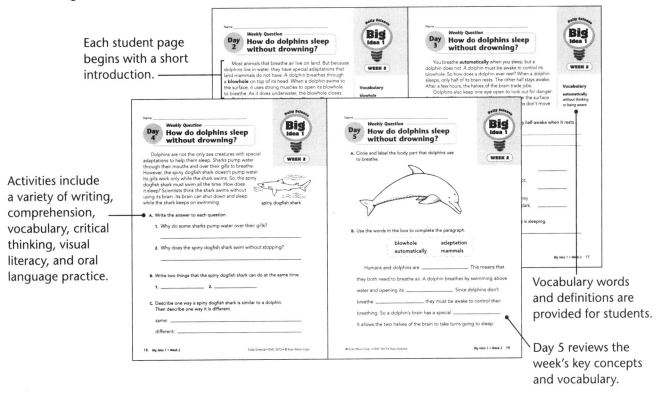

Vocabulary words and definitions are provided for students.

Day 5 reviews the week's key concepts and vocabulary.

Unit Review (Week 5)

Visual Literacy: Students practice skills such as labeling diagrams, reading captions, and sequencing steps in a process.

Hands-on Activity: Students participate in a hands-on learning experience.

Comprehension: Students review key concepts of the unit by answering literal and inferential comprehension questions.

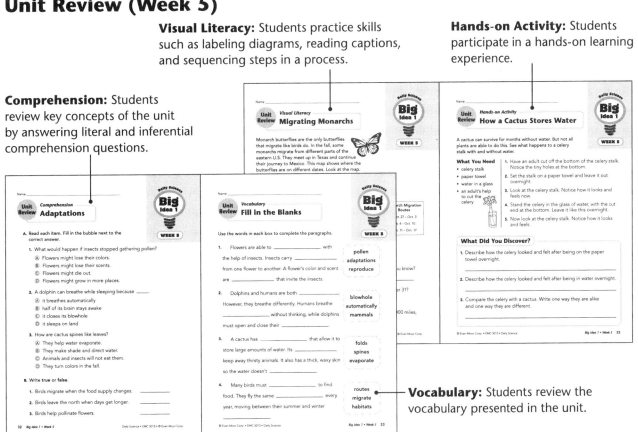

Vocabulary: Students review the vocabulary presented in the unit.

Big Idea 1

Living things have adaptations that help them survive in their environment.

Key Concepts
Adaptations and the Environment

National Standard
Each plant or animal has different structures that serve different functions in growth, survival, and reproduction.

Third-grade students have a basic understanding that some living things live in specific environments. However, students may not understand that the characteristics of living things allow them to thrive in their environment, and that those characteristics may change over time. This Big Idea teaches students that:

→ adaptations help plants reproduce;

→ some animals have adapted their body functions to survive;

→ living things develop ways to protect themselves; and

→ adaptations of animal behavior help them to survive.

Teacher Background

Every living thing has adaptations that help it protect itself, survive conditions in its habitat, find food, grow, and reproduce. When there are changes in an environment, living things in that environment respond in one of three ways: they adapt, they leave, or they become extinct.

Some adaptations develop over millions of years. Others are produced in just a few generations. Adaptations may help two living things support each other, such as plants and the animals that help pollinate them. Some adaptations help an animal or plant protect itself from predators. Still other adaptations involve an animal's body functions or behavior, such as migration. Each living thing has multiple adaptations that help it survive and grow in its environment. As environments change, so do adaptations.

For specific background information on each week's concepts, refer to the notes on pp. 8, 14, 20, and 26.

Unit Overview

WEEK 1: Why do flowers have different colors and scents?

Connection to the Big Idea: Students learn that adaptations help plants reproduce.

Students first learn about pollination. Then they learn that flowers have different colors and scents to attract animals that feed on the flowers' pollen and nectar. Students discover that the animals carry pollen from one flower to another, helping to pollinate the plants.

Content Vocabulary: *adaptation, pollen, pollinates, reproduce*

WEEK 2: How do dolphins sleep without drowning?

Connection to the Big Idea: Students learn about adaptations that allow dolphins to sleep in the water.

Students learn that dolphins are mammals that are adapted to life in the water. Students discover that a dolphin has an unusual adaptation that lets half its brain sleep while the other half stays awake to control its breathing.

Content Vocabulary: *automatically, blowhole, mammal*

WEEK 3: Why does a cactus have needles?

Connection to the Big Idea: Students learn how a cactus's adaptations help it survive in the desert.

Students discover that cacti have needles, or spines, that protect the plant from being eaten, provide shade, collect water, and protect small animals that help the cactus reproduce. Students also learn about a cactus's other adaptations.

Content Vocabulary: *evaporate, folds, spine*

WEEK 4: Why do birds migrate?

Connection to the Big Idea: Students learn that adaptations in behavior also help living things survive.

Students find out that many birds migrate twice a year, sometimes flying thousands of miles. They discover that the availability of food is the main reason why birds migrate. In addition, students learn that birds migrate to places with plenty of food and few predators in order to reproduce and raise their babies.

Content Vocabulary: *habitat, migrate, predator, route*

WEEK 5: Unit Review

You may choose to do these activities to review the concepts of adaptations and survival.

p. 32: Comprehension Students answer multiple-choice questions about key concepts from the unit.

p. 33: Vocabulary Students fill in vocabulary words in context to show understanding of word meanings.

p. 34: Visual Literacy Students interpret a map depicting the timing and direction of butterfly migration.

p. 35: Hands-on Activity Students conduct an experiment to demonstrate how celery holds water. Instructions and materials are listed on the student page.

Daily Science

Big Idea 1

Living things have adaptations that help them survive in their environment.

Week 1

Why do flowers have different colors and scents?

This week, students learn about plants' adaptations. Since plants cannot move, they have developed adaptations to enable them to reproduce. Colors and scents are examples of these adaptations. Different animals are attracted to different colors and scents. They create a symbiotic relationship with flowering plants. Plants offer birds and insects food and sometimes shelter, and the animals in turn help pollinate the plants.

Day One

Vocabulary: *adaptation, reproduce*

Materials: pictures of regional flowers

Distribute page 9 and introduce the vocabulary. Have volunteers read the introduction aloud. Then point out the pictures on the page and have volunteers read the name of each flower. Ask: **Have you ever seen any of these flowers? What color were they? What did they smell like?** Have students complete the first two activities. For activity C, show students pictures of local flowers and have them pick one to describe.

Day Two

Vocabulary: *pollen, pollinates*

Distribute page 10 and introduce the vocabulary. Then have volunteers read the introduction aloud. Point out that the words *pollen* and *pollinates* have related meanings and that knowing the word *pollen* can help them remember *pollinates*. Then direct students to complete activities A and B. For the oral activity, pair students or discuss possible answers as a group. (e.g., Wind and water carry pollen; people pollinate plants that they want to grow; etc.)

Day Three

Distribute page 11 and have volunteers read the introduction aloud. Have students name some of their favorite foods and describe how the foods look or smell. (e.g., spicy, juicy, sweet, gooey, etc.) Say: **Just like we do, animals prefer different kinds of food.** Then read the descriptions of the plants and animals pictured on the page and have students complete the activity. Review the answers together.

Day Four

Materials: pictures of a rafflesia (optional)

Ask: **Can you imagine a flower that stinks?** Distribute page 12 and read the introduction together. If you have them, show students pictures of the rafflesia. Have students complete activity A. For activity B, say: **The rafflesia uses scent to attract insects, but some plants and animals use scent to keep others away.** If necessary, help students brainstorm ideas before writing their responses. (e.g., skunk, stink bug, eucalyptus, etc.)

Day Five

Tell students they will review everything they have learned about plants' adaptations. Have them complete page 13. Go over the answers together.

Name _____

Day 1

Weekly Question

Why do flowers have different colors and scents?

Nine out of every ten plants on Earth have flowers. Flowers are beautiful to look at and to smell, but they are also important to the plant because they make seeds. Plants need seeds to **reproduce**, or make new plants.

The sizes, colors, and scents of flowers are all different. Scientists call these differences **adaptations**. Adaptations help plants grow and survive.

Vocabulary

adaptation
a change in a living thing that helps it live in its environment

reproduce
to produce offspring, or babies

rose   aster   tulip   daffodil

A. Name two adaptations that flowers have.

1. _____   **2.** _____

B. Write a vocabulary word to complete each sentence.

1. Seeds help plants make new plants, or _____.

2. A flower's color is one _____ that helps the plant survive.

C. Describe a flower that grows where you live. What color is it? What does it smell like?

_____

_____

Name _____

 Day 2

Weekly Question

Why do flowers have different colors and scents?

Flowers make seeds when **pollen** travels from the male part of a flower to the female part. Insects help carry pollen from one flower to another. When an insect lands on a flower, pollen sticks to the insect. When the insect visits another flower, some of the pollen falls off its body and **pollinates** that flower.

A. Number the events below in the correct order.

____ The bee flies to another flower.

____ The bee lands on a flower to eat and drink.

____ The flower makes seeds.

____ Pollen falls off the bee.

____ Pollen sticks to the bee.

B. Write the vocabulary words to complete the sentence.

When a bee carries _____ from one flower

to another, the bee _____ the flower.

 Talk

How else might pollen get from one flower to another? Discuss it with a partner.

Vocabulary

pollen
a grainy, yellow dust made by the male part of a flower

pollinates
brings pollen from one flower to another flower

Name _____

Day 3

Weekly Question

Why do flowers have different colors and scents?

Because flowers need help getting pollen from one to another, they use color and scent to attract animals. Insects and birds eat pollen and drink nectar (NEK-tuhr), a sweet liquid that flowers make. A flower's color and scent tell these animals that food is available. Different colors and scents invite different animals.

Use the clues to decide which flower invites which animal. Then draw a line to connect them.

Violets are purple flowers with a sweet scent.

Moths are active at night. They like flowers with strong scents.

Honeysuckles open at night. They have a very strong scent.

Bees like colors, but they can't see red. They also like sweet scents.

The bright red hibiscus doesn't have much scent, but it has lots of nectar.

Hummingbirds like red flowers with lots of nectar.

Name _____

Day 4

Weekly Question

Why do flowers have different colors and scents?

Rafflesia (ruh-FLEE-zhuh) is a kind of plant that lives in the rainforest. Its most unusual adaptation is its scent. A rafflesia flower smells and looks like rotting meat. Its horrible smell invites flies. Flies help pollinate the rafflesia by carrying pollen from flower to flower.

rafflesia

A. Write **true** or **false**.

1. All flowers must smell good to attract animals. _____

2. The rafflesia smells and looks bad to keep other plants from growing near it. _____

3. Flies are attracted to rotting meat more than they are attracted to sweet-smelling flowers. _____

B. Do you know of any other plants or animals that use bad smells to survive? Describe them below.

_____

_____

Name _____

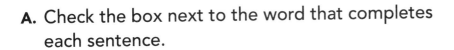

Day 5

Weekly Question

Why do flowers have different colors and scents?

A. Check the box next to the word that completes each sentence.

1. Colors and scents are examples of _____.

☐ nectar   ☐ pollen   ☐ adaptations   ☐ plants

2. Insects and birds carry _____ to flowers.

☐ pollen   ☐ flies   ☐ scents   ☐ seeds

3. Without _____, a plant couldn't reproduce.

☐ nectar   ☐ pollen   ☐ flies   ☐ hummingbirds

B. Use the words in the box to complete the paragraph.

> pollen   adaptations   survive

Different colors and scents are _____ that help

plants attract animals. The animals carry _____

from flower to flower, which helps the plants make seeds. Without

seeds, the plants couldn't _____.

C. Why are flowers an important part of a plant? Explain what they do.

_____

_____

Living things have adaptations that help them survive in their environment.

Week 2

How do dolphins sleep without drowning?

This week, students learn about a dolphin's adaptations. Dolphins are mammals, and like all mammals they breathe air. Even though they can remain underwater for long periods of time, they must return to the surface to breathe. Dolphins need sleep, too, but if they fell into a deep sleep, they would drown. So their brains have a unique adaptation. Half of their brain goes to sleep while the other half stays awake. In this way, dolphins can rest without drowning.

Day One Vocabulary: *mammal*	Ask students to share what they know about dolphins. Distribute page 15, introduce the vocabulary word, and read the introduction together. Model filling in the chart for activity A by completing the first row. Then have students finish the chart and complete activity B on their own. For activity C, brainstorm responses, such as a bed, quiet, a night light, etc. Then ask: **What do you think a dolphin needs to sleep well? What challenges does it face?** (staying safe, getting air)
Day Two Vocabulary: *blowhole*	Ask students to name the parts of the body we use when we breathe. (nose, mouth, throat, lungs, etc.) Ask: **What body parts do humans use when they swim?** (arms, legs, lungs, etc.) Distribute page 16 and introduce the vocabulary word. Then have volunteers read the introduction aloud. Have students complete the activities. Review the answers together.
Day Three Vocabulary: *automatically*	Introduce the vocabulary word by asking: **Which do you do automatically in your sleep—breathe or play?** (breathe) Elicit other things our bodies do automatically (blink, keep heart beating, digest food, etc.) versus things we have to think about (run, eat, talk, etc.). Then say: **Dolphins can't breathe or swim automatically, but they have figured out a way to rest.** Distribute page 17 and read the introduction together. Have students complete the activities. Review the answers together.
Day Four	Distribute page 18 and have volunteers read the introduction aloud. Explain that sharks are types of fish. They breathe by taking in water and using their gills to get oxygen out of the water. Then have students complete activities A and B. For activity C, draw a Venn diagram on the board and have students work as a group to think of similarities and differences between a dolphin and a spiny dogfish shark.
Day Five	Tell students they will review everything they have learned about a dolphin's adaptations. Have students complete page 19. Go over the answers together.

Name _____

Day 1

Weekly Question

How do dolphins sleep without drowning?

Dolphins are **mammals**, just like we are. Mammals are alike in certain ways. Both dolphins and humans breathe air and need regular sleep. Their babies are born alive instead of hatching from eggs. Dolphins and humans both have a backbone. However, dolphins do not have a nose like we do. And, instead of four limbs, they have flippers and a tail.

Vocabulary

mammal
a kind of warm-blooded animal that has a backbone

A. Read each feature. Write **yes** or **no** to tell if dolphins or humans have or need that feature.

	Dolphin	Human
Has arms and legs		
Breathes air		
Needs regular sleep		
Has a nose		

B. Check the box next to the body part dolphins and humans both have.

☐ arms   ☐ nose   ☐ backbone

C. Write three things that YOU need in order to sleep well.

1. _____ 2. _____ 3. _____

Name _____

Day 2

Weekly Question

How do dolphins sleep without drowning?

Most animals that breathe air live on land. But because dolphins live in water, they have special adaptations that land mammals do not have. A dolphin breathes through a **blowhole** on top of its head. When a dolphin swims to the surface, it uses strong muscles to open its blowhole to breathe. As it dives underwater, the blowhole closes.

Dolphins also have a tail and two flippers. They swim through the water by moving their tails and steering with their flippers.

Vocabulary

blowhole
an opening on the top of the head through which a dolphin breathes

A. Explain how these adaptations help a dolphin live in water.

1. blowhole _____

2. tail _____

3. flippers _____

B. Study the dolphin diagram below. Use the words in the box to label each part of the dolphin.

blowhole

tail

flippers

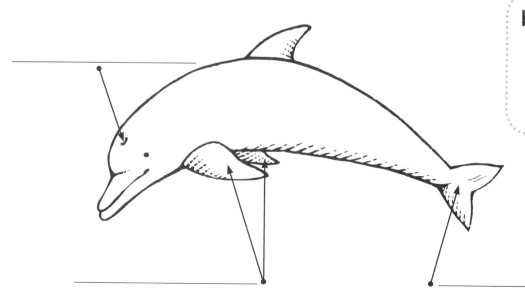

Name _____

Day 3

Weekly Question

How do dolphins sleep without drowning?

You breathe **automatically** when you sleep, but a dolphin does not. A dolphin must be awake to control its blowhole. So how does a dolphin ever rest? When a dolphin sleeps, only half of its brain rests. The other half stays awake. After a few hours, the halves of the brain trade jobs.

Dolphins also keep one eye open to look out for danger. And they still have to swim so they can be near the surface of the water. But when they're resting, dolphins don't move very fast.

Vocabulary

automatically
without thinking or being aware

A. Write two reasons why a dolphin must stay half-awake when it rests.

1. _____

2. _____

B. Write **true** or **false**.

1. Dolphins breathe automatically.   _____

2. If both halves of a dolphin's brain slept,
the dolphin couldn't swim.   _____

3. Dolphins keep one eye open when they
sleep because they are afraid of the dark.   _____

C. Describe one thing a dolphin does while it is sleeping.

_____

Name _____

Day 4

Weekly Question

How do dolphins sleep without drowning?

Dolphins are not the only sea creatures with special adaptations to help them sleep. Sharks pump water through their mouths and over their gills to breathe. However, the spiny dogfish shark doesn't pump water. Its gills work only while the shark swims. So, the spiny dogfish shark must swim all the time. How does it sleep? Scientists think the shark swims without using its brain. Its brain can shut down and sleep while the shark keeps on swimming.

spiny dogfish shark

A. Write the answer to each question.

   1. Why do some sharks pump water over their gills?

   _____

   2. Why does the spiny dogfish shark swim without stopping?

   _____

B. Write two things that the spiny dogfish shark can do at the same time.

   1. _____   **2.** _____

C. Describe one way a spiny dogfish shark is similar to a dolphin. Then describe one way it is different.

   same: _____

   different: _____

Name _____

Day 5

How do dolphins sleep without drowning?

Daily Science

Big Idea 1

WEEK 2

A. Circle and label the body part that dolphins use to breathe.

B. Use the words in the box to complete the paragraph.

> blowhole   adaptation
>
> automatically mammals

Humans and dolphins are _____. This means that

they both need to breathe air. A dolphin breathes by swimming above

water and opening its _____. Since dolphins don't

breathe _____, they must be awake to control their

breathing. So a dolphin's brain has a special _____.

It allows the two halves of the brain to take turns going to sleep.

Big Idea 1

Living things have adaptations that help them survive in their environment.

Week 3

Why does a cactus have needles?

This week, students learn about a cactus's adaptations. In order to survive in a desert environment, cacti have many adaptations. Instead of broad, flat leaves, cacti have needles, or spines. Spines create shade for the cactus, preventing water loss from sun exposure. They help the plant collect water from fog and dew, directing it to drip on the long, shallow roots below. The spines also deter animals that are seeking water, and provide shelter for some birds, such as mourning doves, who nest in cacti for protection.

Day One

Vocabulary: *evaporate*

Activate prior knowledge by asking students to list features of a desert. (dry, hot, sunny, sandy, few plants and animals, etc.) Distribute page 21 and introduce the vocabulary word. Then have volunteers read the introduction aloud. Point out the picture of the cactus and ask students to describe what they see. (spines, ridges or folds in the skin, flowers, etc.) Then have students complete the activities. Review the answers together.

Day Two

Vocabulary: *spine*

Distribute page 22 and introduce the vocabulary word, pointing out the difference in meaning from the one students are probably familiar with. (backbone) Discuss the qualities of a cactus's spines. (sharp, thin, hard, etc.) Then ask students to think what the spines might be good for. (protection) Have volunteers read the introduction aloud and then have students complete the activities. Review the answers together.

Day Three

Materials: pictures of a cactus and a porcupine (optional)

Distribute page 23. Have volunteers read the introduction aloud. Then point out the picture of the cholla on the page and brainstorm with students other plants that have similar adaptations. (Roses have thorns; bark protects trees; burrs stick to socks; etc.) Have students complete the activities. For activity B, give students background information about porcupines, if needed. Then review the answers together.

Day Four

Vocabulary: *folds*

Distribute page 24 and introduce the vocabulary word. Then have volunteers read the introduction aloud. You may also want to read aloud the adaptations and conditions listed in activity A. Then have students complete the activities. Review the answers together.

Day Five

Tell students they will review everything they have learned about a cactus's adaptations. Have students complete page 25. Then go over the answers together.

Name _____

Day 1

Weekly Question

Why does a cactus have needles?

It is difficult for living things to survive in deserts because most deserts are dry and hot. It may not rain for months. When it does rain, the hot, dry weather makes the water quickly **evaporate**. Without clouds, there is little shade from the sun. A desert plant, such as a cactus, must adapt to the harsh desert conditions in order to stay alive and grow.

Vocabulary

evaporate
to change from a liquid to a gas

A. What are two things that make life in the desert difficult?

1. _____

2. _____

B. Read each question. Check the box next to the correct answer.

1. Based on what you know about the desert, which of these animals could survive in the desert?

   ☐ a kangaroo rat that needs little water

   ☐ a white-tailed deer that eats pine tree needles

   ☐ a polar bear with thick fur to protect it from the cold

2. Which one would cause water in a cup to evaporate faster?

   ☐ leaving it by the window on a cool, cloudy day

   ☐ leaving it by the window on a warm, sunny day

Name _____

Weekly Question

Day 2

Why does a cactus have needles?

The needles on a cactus, called **spines**, are actually a kind of leaf. The spine is an adaptation of a regular leaf to help the cactus survive in the desert. Just as there are different kinds of leaves, there are different kinds of cactus spines. Some help the cactus collect rain. These long spines direct water to the cactus's roots.

Other kinds of spines grow thickly over the cactus. They protect it from the sun and help keep the cactus from drying out. Water is less likely to evaporate if the sun is not shining directly on the cactus's skin.

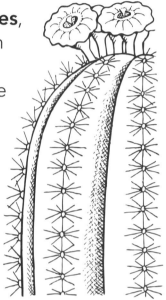

saguaro cactus

Vocabulary

spine
a stiff, sharp needle of a cactus

A. Check the box next to the word that completes each sentence.

1. Spines are an adaptation of _____.

☐ leaves   ☐ roots   ☐ flowers

2. Some spines on a cactus help collect _____.

☐ sunlight   ☐ water   ☐ sand

3. Some kinds of spines protect the cactus from _____.

☐ rain   ☐ cold   ☐ sunlight

B. Predict what would probably happen to the leaves of a regular plant in the desert.

_____

Name _____

Day 3

Weekly Question

Why does a cactus have needles?

Spines do more than help a cactus survive in desert conditions. They protect the cactus from animals looking for a juicy meal. The spines break off easily and will stick in an animal's mouth if it tries to eat the cactus.

Some spines also help the cactus reproduce. For example, the jumping cholla (CHOY-ah) breaks apart easily when an animal brushes against it. The spines make the broken-off piece stick to the passing animal. When the cactus piece finally drops off, it grows roots and becomes a new plant!

jumping cholla

A. Explain how animals help the jumping cholla reproduce.

_____

_____

B. A porcupine is an animal that has sharp needles, called quills, on its body. How do you think a porcupine's quills might be similar to a cactus's spines?

_____

C. Write **true** or **false**.

1. A cactus's spines are sharp like needles.   _____

2. A cactus uses its spines to attract animals.   _____

Name _____

Weekly Question

Why does a cactus have needles?

Spines aren't the only adaptations a cactus has for surviving in the desert. Some cacti have **folds** that can swell and store hundreds of gallons of water. Their roots are shallow and spread far from the plant. The roots are ready to drink up even the smallest amount of rain. The thick, waxy skin of the cactus keeps the water inside from evaporating.

Vocabulary

folds
bends or ridges that allow something to get bigger

A. Draw a line to match how each adaptation helps the cactus survive in the desert.

Adaptation	Desert Condition
folds that swell and store water •	• heat that causes water to quickly evaporate after it lands
shallow roots that absorb rain quickly •	• a lot of sunlight without shade
thick skin that protects the cactus •	• long periods of time without rain

B. Look at the diagram.
Label the **folds**, **roots**, and **flower**.

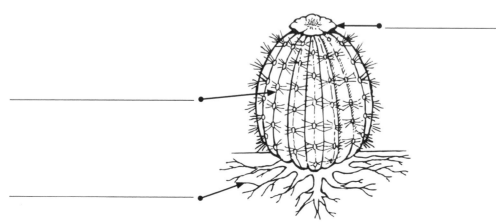

Daily Science • EMC 5013 • © Evan-Moor Corp.

Name ______________________________

Daily Science Big Idea 1

WEEK 3

Day 5

Weekly Question

Why does a cactus have needles?

A. Describe two jobs that a cactus's spines can do to help the cactus survive in the desert.

1. ______________________________

2. ______________________________

B. Use the words in the box to complete the paragraph.

evaporate survive folds spines

A cactus is adapted to ______________ in a hot, dry desert. It stores up water and uses the water slowly. The thick, waxy skin of the cactus helps make sure that the water doesn't ______________. Sharp ______________ protect the plant. They also help it collect water. The ______________ of the cactus allow it to store as much water as possible.

C. Which analogy is correct? Check the box next to it.

- ☐ **Spines** are to **cactus** as **flowers** are to **plant.**
- ☐ **Spines** are to **cactus** as **roots** are to **plant.**
- ☐ **Spines** are to **cactus** as **leaves** are to **plant.**

Daily Science

Big Idea 1

Living things have adaptations that help them survive in their environment.

Week 4

Why do birds migrate?

This week, students will learn that birds migrate mainly because of changes in food supply and habitat during seasonal changes. In northern locations, there are plenty of insects and vegetation during spring and summer. These places provide a good habitat for many kinds of birds to reproduce and raise their young. As winter approaches, food becomes harder to find and daylight lessens, so birds head south to areas where food and sunshine are more plentiful. Even though scientists have extensively studied different migratory birds, they are still not sure exactly how birds sense fewer daylight hours and know it is time to migrate.

Day One

Vocabulary: *migrate, route*

Materials: globe; pictures of an Arctic tern and other migratory birds

Distribute page 27 and introduce the vocabulary. For *route*, reinforce meaning by inviting students to explain the route they take to school. Then have volunteers read the introduction aloud. Show students the pictures of birds. Use a globe to show students how far the Arctic tern flies. Then have students complete activity A. For activity B, distribute crayons and guide students through the map before having them complete the activity.

Day Two

Vocabulary: *habitat*

Materials: globe

Distribute page 28 and introduce the vocabulary word. Explain that an animal's habitat can change with the seasons. Have volunteers read the introduction aloud. Show students the Northern and Southern Hemispheres on the globe and explain that because of Earth's tilt on its axis, winter in North America means it is summer in South America. Then have students complete activity A. Discuss activity B as a group before having students answer the questions. Review the answers together.

Day Three

Vocabulary: *predator*

Distribute page 29 and introduce the vocabulary word. Say: **Foxes, bobcats, and hawks are examples of predators that eat birds.** Have volunteers read the introduction aloud. Then have students complete activity A. For activity B, guide students through the chart, modeling how to read each row. Then have students answer the questions independently.

Day Four

Distribute page 30. Have volunteers read the introduction aloud. If necessary, explain what Earth's magnetic field is. (the magnetic field surrounding Earth) Then read aloud each question. Have students write their answers and then share their responses, explaining their thinking. For the oral activity, pair students or discuss as a group. Explain that scientists often choose to study the questions that most interest them.

Day Five

Tell students they will review everything they have learned about birds' migration. Have them complete page 31. Go over the answers together.

Name _____

Day 1

Weekly Question

Why do birds migrate?

As the seasons change, some animals **migrate**, or move from one place to another. Birds are good at migrating. They can fly anywhere! Some birds travel only a few hundred miles, while others take **routes** that cover thousands of miles. The Arctic tern is the long-distance champ. It leaves its nesting place in the Arctic and migrates to Antarctica. That's a trip of more than 10,000 miles!

A. Write **true** or **false**.

1. Birds often migrate when the seasons change. _____

2. **Migrating** always means flying to Antarctica. _____

3. Birds follow routes, but people don't. _____

Vocabulary

migrate
to travel from one place to another when the seasons change

route
a path or course

B. Look at the map. Color the arrows that show the route of the Arctic tern. Then complete the caption below.

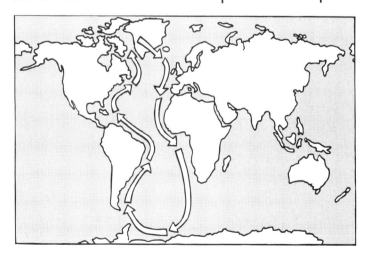

This is the _____ of the Arctic tern when it _____.

Name _____

Why do birds migrate?

The main reason birds leave their **habitats** and migrate is to go where the food will be when the seasons change. When fall comes in the north, the daytime gets shorter, and flowers and insects disappear. Birds that feed on nectar, berries, seeds, and insects need a new supply of food. They head south, where it is often warmer and the days are longer.

Other kinds of birds live in wet **habitats**, such as marshes, rivers, or lakes, that dry up during certain times of the year. These birds will migrate when their habitat becomes dry.

Vocabulary

habitat
the natural home of an animal or plant

A. Answer the questions below.

1. Do you think most birds prefer longer, warmer days or

   longer, cooler nights? _____

2. What are two foods that birds eat?

   _____ and _____

3. Why do most birds migrate? _____

B. During the summer in Maryland, hummingbirds eat nectar while hawks eat small animals, such as mice and lizards. Which bird do you think will migrate in the winter? Which bird will stay? Explain your answer.

_____

_____

Name _____

Day 3

Weekly Question

Why do birds migrate?

You might wonder why birds don't stay in the south all the time. They have good reasons for migrating back to the north. There are good places for them to reproduce and raise their young. There are often fewer **predators** in the north, too. Birds return during the spring because plants start growing again. And there are also more hours of daylight during summer months. This means there's more time to find food.

Vocabulary

predator
an animal that hunts other animals for food

A. List three reasons why birds return to the north in spring.

1. _____

2. _____

3. _____

B. The chart below shows when some birds return to the north and where they go. Use the chart to answer the questions.

Bird	When It Returns	Where It Returns To
Marsh Wren	May 10	New York
Song Sparrow	February 19	Maryland
Yellow Warbler	April 3	Louisiana

1. Which bird returns the earliest? _____

2. What state does a bird return to during April? _____

3. Do all birds migrate north at the same time? _____

 Day 4 *Weekly Question*

Why do birds migrate?

How birds migrate is still a mystery to scientists. One question is how the birds have enough energy to fly for so long. Scientists think that as the days grow shorter, birds' bodies store up fat for the long trip.

Another question is how birds find their way. Scientists believe that birds can find their routes because they have something in their bodies that acts like a compass. This adaptation help birds use the sun, the stars, and Earth's magnetic field to find their way.

Read each question. Then write your answer.

1. Do you think birds that have to travel a long way store up a little fat or a lot of fat? Explain why you think so.

   _____

   _____

2. Some birds don't migrate. Do you think these birds have the same adaptations as migrating birds do to help them find routes? Why or why not?

   _____

   _____

 Talk

Which one would be more interesting to discover, knowing how birds decide when it is time to migrate or knowing how birds figure out their route? Why? Discuss it with a partner.

Name _____

Day 5

Weekly Question

Why do birds migrate?

A. What happens to birds when the days get shorter? Fill in the bubble next to the correct answer.

Ⓐ They stop eating.   Ⓒ They lay eggs.

Ⓑ They store up fat.   Ⓓ They build nests.

B. Name one reason why birds migrate. Write a complete sentence.

_____

_____

C. Use the words in the box to complete the paragraph.

> **predators   reproduce   migrate   habitat**

When the seasons change, many birds _____

to find a better supply of food. Some fly for thousands of miles.

One reason birds return to their homes in the spring is to

_____. They need a _____ with

plenty of food to feed their young. There may also be less danger

from _____.

Name _____

Unit Review *Comprehension*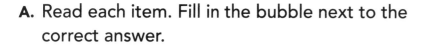

Adaptations

A. Read each item. Fill in the bubble next to the correct answer.

1. What would happen if insects stopped gathering pollen?

   Ⓐ Flowers might lose their colors.

   Ⓑ Flowers might lose their scents.

   Ⓒ Flowers might die out.

   Ⓓ Flowers might grow in more places.

2. A dolphin can breathe while sleeping because _____.

   Ⓐ it breathes automatically

   Ⓑ half of its brain stays awake

   Ⓒ it closes its blowhole

   Ⓓ it sleeps on land

3. How are cactus spines like leaves?

   Ⓐ They help water evaporate.

   Ⓑ They make shade and direct water.

   Ⓒ Animals and insects will not eat them.

   Ⓓ They turn colors in the fall.

B. Write **true** or **false**.

1. Birds migrate when the food supply changes. _____

2. Birds leave the north when days get longer. _____

3. Birds help pollinate flowers. _____

Name _____

Unit Review

Vocabulary

Fill in the Blanks

Use the words in each box to complete the paragraphs.

1. Flowers are able to _____ with the help of insects. Insects carry _____ from one flower to another. A flower's color and scent are _____ that invite the insects.

pollen
adaptations
reproduce

2. Dolphins and humans are both _____. However, they breathe differently. Humans breathe _____ without thinking, while dolphins must open and close their _____.

blowhole
automatically
mammals

3. A cactus has _____ that allow it to store large amounts of water. Its _____ keep away thirsty animals. It also has a thick, waxy skin so the water doesn't _____.

folds
spines
evaporate

4. Many birds must _____ to find food. They fly the same _____ every year, moving between their summer and winter _____.

routes
migrate
habitats

Name _____

Monarch butterflies are the only butterflies that migrate like birds do. In the fall, some monarchs migrate from different parts of the eastern U.S. They meet up in Texas and continue their journey to Mexico. This map shows where the butterflies are on different dates. Look at the map. Then answer the questions.

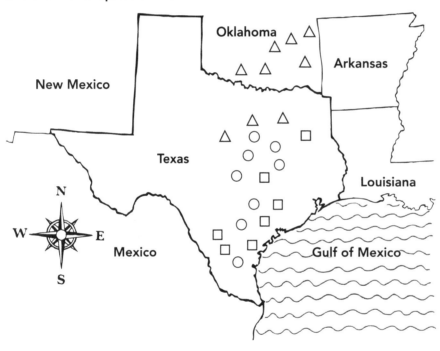

Monarch Migration Routes

△ Sept. 27 – Oct. 3

○ Oct. 4 – Oct. 10

□ Oct. 11 – Oct. 17

1. In which direction are the monarchs traveling? How do you know?

_____

2. What country are the butterflies likely to reach by October 31?

_____

3. If the butterflies fly 100 miles a day and have to travel 3,000 miles,

how long will the trip take them? _____

Name _____

Unit Review

Hands-on Activity

How a Cactus Stores Water

A cactus can survive for months without water. But not all plants are able to do this. See what happens to a celery stalk with and without water.

What You Need

- celery stalk
- paper towel
- water in a glass
- an adult's help to cut the celery

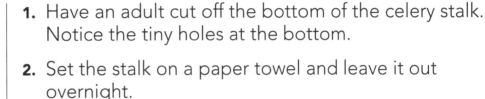

1. Have an adult cut off the bottom of the celery stalk. Notice the tiny holes at the bottom.

2. Set the stalk on a paper towel and leave it out overnight.

3. Look at the celery stalk. Notice how it looks and feels now.

4. Stand the celery in the glass of water, with the cut end at the bottom. Leave it like this overnight.

5. Now look at the celery stalk. Notice how it looks and feels.

What Did You Discover?

1. Describe how the celery looked and felt after being on the paper towel overnight.

   _____

2. Describe how the celery looked and felt after being in water overnight.

   _____

3. Compare the celery with a cactus. Write one way they are alike and one way they are different.

   _____

Plants have many parts.
Each part does a special job.

Key Concept
Plants and Their Parts

National Standard
Each plant or animal has different structures that serve different functions in growth, survival, and reproduction.

By third grade, students should understand that plants have specific parts. But students may not understand how these parts function and work together. This Big Idea teaches students:

→ the role of roots, stems, leaves, flowers, and fruits;

→ how water moves through a plant;

→ the way plants distribute seeds; and

→ the life cycle of plants.

Teacher Background

Like all organisms, plants need food, water, shelter, and the opportunity to reproduce. Without these, no plant could survive. But plants have the additional challenge of being fixed in the ground, so plants cannot move freely within their environment.

Unlike animals, plants cannot hunt or forage for food. Instead, they make their own food. Plants cannot go to a water supply. Instead, they have roots to absorb water and minerals from the soil. Plants spend their time outdoors exposed to the elements but have adaptations that shelter them from harm. Although plants can't move to new environments, they have created clever ways of reproducing and distributing their seeds so that the next generation of plants can spread to new places.

For specific background information on each week's concepts, refer to the notes on pp. 38, 44, 50, and 56.

WEEK 1: What's the difference between a fruit and a vegetable?

Connection to the Big Idea: Fruits come from the pollinated ovaries of flowers, while vegetables can refer to any other edible plant part.

Students learn that a fruit is the part of a plant that contains seeds, and that many things we think of as vegetables are actually fruits. Students then learn that a vegetable is any other edible part of a plant, such as the root, leaf, or stem. Finally, students discover that some other foods come from the seeds of plants.

Content Vocabulary: *fruit, leaves, pollinate, root, seeds, stem, vegetable*

WEEK 2: How do plants get water from roots to leaves?

Connection to the Big Idea: A plant's roots, stem, and leaves move water and nutrients through the plant.

Students learn about diffuse and tap roots, as well as the makeup and job of a plant's stem. Finally, they learn that leaves have pores that release water back into the air.

Content Vocabulary: *absorb, diffuse root, nutrients, pores, tap root*

WEEK 3: Why do dandelions turn white and fluffy?

Connection to the Big Idea: Flowering plants have developed ways of using special parts to spread seeds.

Students learn that a dandelion plant has special adaptations to help it distribute seeds. They then discover that many plants have special seeds that use wind, water, or animals to help them distribute seeds.

Content Vocabulary: *conditions, distribute, parachute, seed coat, seed germ*

WEEK 4: Why do leaves change color in the fall?

Connection to the Big Idea: Leaves change color when chlorophyll disappears and is replaced by reds, oranges, and yellows.

Students learn how chlorophyll and photosynthesis help plants make food. They then discover how plants quit making chlorophyll when winter comes and resume its production in the spring.

Content Vocabulary: *carbon dioxide, cell, chlorophyll, conserving, photosynthesis*

WEEK 5: Unit Review

These activities review key concepts of plant structure and function.

p. 62: Comprehension Students answer multiple-choice questions about key concepts from the unit.

p. 63: Vocabulary Students match vocabulary words from the unit to their definitions and complete cloze sentences.

p. 64: Visual Literacy Students match captions to pictures that show how burr seeds are distributed.

p. 65: Hands-on Activity Students investigate how water moves through a plant by using food coloring and carnations. Review the materials and instructions on the student page ahead of time.

Plants have many parts. Each part does a special job.

Week 1

What's the difference between a fruit and a vegetable?

Most students would probably identify a banana as a fruit and a carrot as a vegetable, but they probably couldn't explain the difference between the two. From a culinary standpoint, fruits contain more sugar and are sweeter. From a scientific standpoint, though, fruits are the parts of a plant that come from the pollinated ovary of a flower and have seeds. Vegetables include all the other edible plant parts, such as stems, roots, and leaves. This means that squash, tomatoes, green beans, and other foods typically thought of as vegetables are actually fruits. And other fruits, such as bananas and some types of grapes, don't have visible seeds due to years of crop selection and farming practices.

Day One

Vocabulary: *fruit, vegetable*

Distribute page 39. Ask: **What do you think makes a fruit a fruit?** Elicit responses and list them on the board. (e.g., tastes sweet, grows on trees, etc.) Then have volunteers read the vocabulary words and their definitions. Next, have volunteers read the introduction aloud. Return to students' responses to the question posed before the reading, and revise the responses as necessary. Then have students complete the activities.

Day Two

Vocabulary: *pollinate, seeds*

Distribute page 40. Say: **All fruit comes from flowers. Without flowers, plants can't make fruit.** Introduce or review the vocabulary and have volunteers read the introduction aloud. Point out the picture on the page and say: **This is how the pomegranate plant grows the fruit we eat.** Discuss the growth sequence before students complete the activities.

Day Three

Vocabulary: *leaves, root, stem*

Distribute page 41 and introduce or review the vocabulary. Then have volunteers read the introduction aloud. Review how each part helps the plant. Write *leaves*, *root*, and *stem* on the board and have volunteers write the names of different vegetables underneath the correct headings. Finally, have students complete the activities independently.

Day Four

Distribute page 42 and have volunteers read the introduction aloud. Brainstorm with students some of the less obvious things made from plants that they eat. (pepper, herbs, pasta, maple syrup, chocolate, etc.) Have students complete the activities, and then invite volunteers to share their responses to activity C.

Day Five

Tell students they will review what they have learned about fruits and vegetables. Have them complete page 43. Review the answers together.

Name _____

Day 1

Weekly Question

What's the difference between a fruit and a vegetable?

You might know that carrots are a **vegetable** and grapes are a **fruit**. But did you know that tomatoes are also a fruit? So are green beans and squash! They are all called fruits because they contain seeds. People eat many different parts of plants and say they are eating vegetables. But if the plant part contains seeds, scientists call it a fruit.

A. Decide whether these foods are fruits or vegetables. Write **F** for fruit or **V** for vegetable below the pictures.

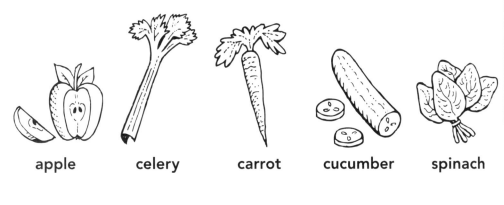

| apple | celery | carrot | cucumber | spinach |

_____   _____   _____   _____   _____

B. Write **true** or **false**.

1. Fruits grow only on trees.   _____

2. You can tell if something is a fruit or a vegetable by its color.   _____

3. Only fruits contain seeds.   _____

Vocabulary

fruit
the part of a flowering plant that includes the seeds

vegetable
a plant part that can be eaten and has no seeds

Name _____

Day 2

Weekly Question

What's the difference between a fruit and a vegetable?

A fruit comes from the flowers of a plant. Fruit grows after a flower is **pollinated** and forms **seeds**. The fruit grows around the seeds and continues to grow even after the flower dies. Fruit tastes good, so birds and other animals carry fruit away to eat. This helps seeds move to new places where they can become new plants.

Vocabulary

pollinate
to bring pollen from one flower to another

seeds
the parts of a plant that can grow into a new plant

A. Complete the sentences. Use words from the paragraph above.

1. Flowers make seeds after they are _____.

2. You will find _____ inside fruit.

3. After a flower dies, the _____ continues growing.

B. Explain how animals and plants that make fruit help each other.

_____

_____

Name _____

Day 3

Weekly Question

What's the difference between a fruit and a vegetable?

People eat other parts of plants besides the fruit. These other parts are called vegetables. Vegetables can be **leaves**, **stems**, or **roots**. Each part of the plant has a special job to help the plant grow. People and animals eat these plant parts so they can grow, too!

A. What part of the plant is each vegetable? Draw a line to match the vegetable to its plant part.

Lettuce
This green vegetable is used in salads.

 •

• **Root**
This absorbs water from the soil.

Potato
This vegetable grows under the ground.

 •

• **Stem**
This connects the roots to the leaves.

Celery
This vegetable grows above the ground.

 •

• **Leaf**
This is usually flat and green and absorbs sunlight.

Vocabulary

leaves
the flat, green plant parts that grow above the ground and absorb sunlight

root
the plant part in the soil that absorbs water from the ground

stem
the part of the plant that connects the roots and the leaves

B. Think of another vegetable. Write its name and the part of the plant it comes from.

Vegetable: _____

Plant part: _____

Name _____

Day 4

Weekly Question

What's the difference between a fruit and a vegetable?

Besides fruits and vegetables, plants make other things that we can eat. Cinnamon is a spice that comes from the bark of a tree. Sugar comes from the stem of the sugarcane plant. Corn is a seed, and bread is made from flour, which is the ground-up seeds of the wheat plant.

A. Identify the plant part that each food comes from. Write **root**, **leaves**, or **seed**.

tea

french fries

popcorn

_____   _____   _____

B. Write **true** or **false**.

1. Plants give us food in many different ways.   _____

2. Only fruits and vegetables come from plants.   _____

3. Spices come from plants.   _____

C. Think about what you have eaten this week. List as many foods as you can think of that came from a plant.

_____   _____   _____

_____   _____   _____

Name _____

Day 5

Weekly Question
What's the difference between a fruit and a vegetable?

A. Use the words in the box to complete the sentences.

> leaves   seeds   stem   pollinated   roots

1. In order for a fruit to grow, a flower must be _____.

2. Fruits are the only plant parts that have _____.

3. Vegetables can be the _____, _____,

or _____ of the plant.

B. Look at the foods pictured below. Write **fruit** or **vegetable** beneath each one.

kiwi   broccoli   squash   potato

_____   _____   _____   _____

C. What makes a plant part a fruit? Fill in the bubble next to the correct answer.

   Ⓐ It must be sweet.   Ⓒ It must have seeds.

   Ⓑ It must have lots of juice.   Ⓓ It must be colorful.

Plants have many parts. Each part does a special job.

Week 2

How do plants get water from roots to leaves?

Students know that all living things need water, and that plants must move water from their roots to their stems and leaves. But students may wonder how this happens. This week they will learn that after water is absorbed by the roots, it moves up through the stem. From the stem, water enters the leaves. Leaves have small holes, called pores, that open and release water back into the air. This is a process called transpiration. The water that is lost this way is replaced by more water entering from the stem, and the movement of water continues. Not only is transpiration the mechanism that drives water from the roots to all parts of the plant, but it plays an important role in the water cycle.

Day One

Ask: **Why do we water plants?** (e.g., so they don't dry up and die) Then ask: **In nature, where does the water for plants usually come from?** (rain) Distribute page 45. Read the introduction aloud and do the first activity together. After students complete activity B, go over the answers together.

Day Two

Vocabulary: *absorb, diffuse root, tap root*

Distribute page 46 and introduce the vocabulary words. Then have volunteers read the introduction aloud. Point out the pictures on the page and discuss the differences between the roots, helping students understand why diffuse roots are good for places such as marshes, swamps, and sand dunes, while tap roots are good for places such as prairies and rocky deserts. Have students complete the activities.

Day Three

Vocabulary: *nutrients*

Materials: blue and green crayons

Distribute page 47 and introduce the vocabulary word. Explain that plants absorb nutrients from the soil and that these nutrients help the plant make the food it needs to survive. Have volunteers read the introduction aloud. Distribute crayons and direct students to complete the activities. If needed, read aloud the question for activity C and brainstorm with students good sources of nutrients. (vegetables, milk, etc.)

Day Four

Vocabulary: *pores*

Materials: sponge

Distribute page 48 and introduce the vocabulary word. Then have volunteers read the introduction aloud. Show students the pores on the sponge and explain that pores on a leaf look similar but are much smaller and don't absorb water the way a sponge does. Have students complete activities A and B. For the oral activity, pair students or discuss as a group. (Our pores release water when we sweat, but it is to keep us cool, not move water through our bodies.)

Day Five

Tell students they will review everything they have learned about how plants move water. Have them complete page 49. Then go over the answers together.

Name _____

Day 1

Weekly Question
How do plants get water from roots to leaves?

Every living thing needs water in order to grow and survive. The water that plants need usually comes from rain falling on the ground and soaking into the soil. A plant's roots are able to get water. But the leaves and stems need water, too. So, since water can't move on its own, the different plant parts must work together to move the water.

A. Look at the diagram. Draw arrows to show the path that water takes as it travels from the air to the leaves of a plant.

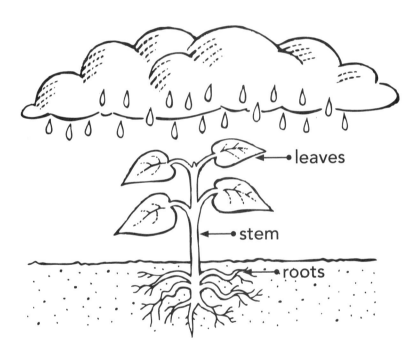

leaves

stem

roots

B. Write the answer to each question.

1. Which part of the plant gets water from the soil? _____

2. Which part of the plant is the last to get water? _____

3. Why do plants need water? _____

Name _____

Day 2
Weekly Question
How do plants get water from roots to leaves?

All roots **absorb** water from the ground. But not all plants have the same kind of roots. Some plants have **tap roots** that grow deep into the ground. Tap roots are good for finding water buried deep below the surface. Plants that live in dry areas with hard dirt often have tap roots. Other plants have **diffuse roots**. These roots spread out far and are good for making sure a plant is strongly supported. Plants that grow in mud or sand often have diffuse roots.

Vocabulary

absorb
to soak up

diffuse root
a type of shallow root that spreads out far

tap root
a type of root that is long and extends deep into the ground

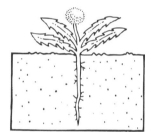
tap root

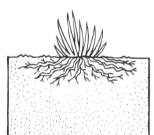
diffuse root

A. Use the vocabulary words to complete each sentence.

1. You could find _____ roots close to the surface.

2. A _____ root is best for finding water deep underground.

3. Plants have parts to _____ water and minerals from the soil.

B. Write which kind of root would work best for the places described below.

1. a wet, soft marsh _____

2. a dry, rocky prairie _____

Name _____

Weekly Question

Day 3

How do plants get water from roots to leaves?

Water that is absorbed by a plant's roots must get to all the cells in the plant. The plant's stem helps with this job. A plant's stem has two parts. The outside of the stem is made from tough fibers that protect it. The inside of the stem is made of long tubes. These tubes move the water and **nutrients** upward from the roots.

A. This diagram shows part of a stem. Use blue to color where the water and nutrients travel. Use green to color the part of the stem that protects the plant.

Vocabulary

nutrients
substances found in soil that help a living thing stay healthy

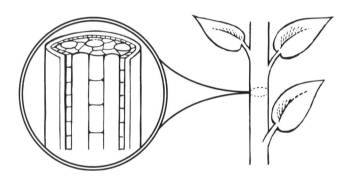

B. Use words from the paragraph above to complete each sentence.

1. Water and _____ move from the roots

   to the leaves through the plant's _____.

2. The outside of the stem _____ the stem, while

   long _____ inside the stem move water upward.

C. A plant's nutrients come from the soil. How do YOU get nutrients? Name two things that you get nutrients from.

1. _____   2. _____

Name _____

Day 4

Weekly Question

How do plants get water from roots to leaves?

Water reaches the leaves of a plant by moving up the plant's stem. But the journey doesn't end there. Water returns to the air through tiny holes in the leaves called **pores**. The pores open and close, letting water escape. Now there are empty spaces in the leaves. Water moves up the stem to fill those spaces. If the pores did not open and let the water out, water would not move through the plant.

Vocabulary

pores
tiny holes in leaves that can open and close

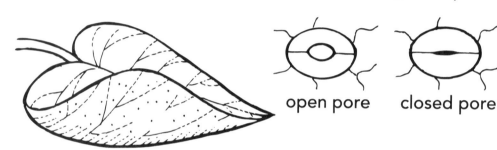

open pore   closed pore

A. Write **true** or **false**.

1. A plant only needs roots to move water.   _____

2. The pores are located in a plant's leaves.   _____

3. The main purpose of pores is to let in light.   _____

B. A leaf's pores do not stay open all the time. Why do you think that is?

_____

 Talk

Your skin has pores, just like a leaf does. How might your pores be the same as a leaf's? Discuss it with a partner.

Name _____

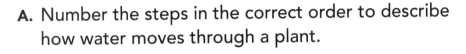

Day 5

Weekly Question

How do plants get water from roots to leaves?

A. Number the steps in the correct order to describe how water moves through a plant.

____ Water moves into the leaves.

____ The ground absorbs water from rain.

____ Water escapes into the air through pores in the leaves.

____ The roots absorb water from the soil.

____ Water moves from the roots up the stem of the plant.

B. Under each plant, write whether it has a **tap root** or a **diffuse root**. Circle the roots.

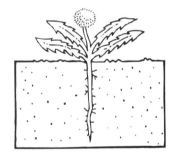   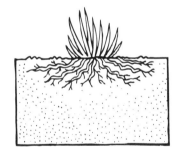

_____   _____

C. Write **true** or **false**.

1. A stem's main job is to move water and nutrients.   _____

2. Pores in leaves let water escape.   _____

3. Only a plant's leaves need water.   _____

Big Idea 2

Plants have many parts. Each part does a special job.

Week 3

Why do dandelions turn white and fluffy?

Students may know that plants reproduce by making seeds, but this week they will learn that making seeds isn't enough. In order to spread, plants must have a way to distribute their seeds. Dandelions have developed seeds that are distributed by the wind. Other seeds are distributed by water or are scattered by animals. Plants have adopted these strategies so that their seeds can find the right conditions of soil, water, and sunlight to grow.

Day One Vocabulary: *distribute*	Distribute page 51 and introduce the vocabulary word. Before reading the introduction aloud, activate prior knowledge by asking students where they have seen dandelions. (lawns, playgrounds, sidewalks, etc.) Guide students through activity A, helping them speculate about where the dandelion seeds are. Then have students complete activity B. Review the answers together.
Day Two Vocabulary: *conditions,* *parachute*	Distribute page 52 and introduce the vocabulary. Have volunteers read the introduction aloud. Develop the meaning of *conditions* by describing the conditions outside (cool or warm, cloudy or sunny, etc.). Then point out the parachute and seed in the picture and have students confirm their speculations from yesterday. You may also want to discuss how a dandelion's parachute is like a parachute that a skydiver uses. (They both float in the air and carry something.) Then have students complete activities A and B. For activity C, consider discussing the question as a class and then having students write their responses. Review the answers together.
Day Three Vocabulary: *seed coat,* *seed germ*	Distribute page 53 and introduce the vocabulary. Explain that the seed coat is like armor that the seed germ, the tiny plant inside the seed, wears. Have volunteers read the introduction aloud, and then have students complete activity A. For activity B, consider pairing students to discuss possible answers.
Day Four	Distribute page 54 and have volunteers read the introduction aloud. If needed, read aloud the sentences in the activity or have volunteers take turns reading them aloud. Then review the answers together.
Day Five	Tell students they will review everything they have learned about seeds. Distribute page 55. When students have finished, review the answers together.

Name _____

Day 1

Weekly Question

Why do dandelions turn white and fluffy?

In spring, yellow-headed dandelions seem to pop up everywhere—along roadsides, in the cracks of sidewalks, and on grassy lawns. Where do the dandelions come from? We know that new plants grow from seeds, but how did the dandelion seeds get to all these different places?

If you have ever blown on a dandelion after the flower has turned white and fluffy, you can guess how the wind helps dandelions **distribute** their seeds.

Vocabulary

distribute
to scatter

A. Look at the dandelion flowers below. Where do you think the seeds are? Circle and label them.

B. Use the words in the box to complete the sentences.

> distribute   flower   seed

1. A _____ can grow into a new plant.

2. Dandelions use the wind to _____ their seeds.

3. A dandelion _____ produces seeds.

Name _____

Day 2

Weekly Question

Why do dandelions turn white and fluffy?

Every dandelion seed is attached to a fine white hair called a **parachute**. The parachute catches the wind and carries the seed through the air. This way, seeds can travel to new places where they can grow. However, a dandelion seed won't grow until it finds the right **conditions**. It needs soil, sunlight, and water.

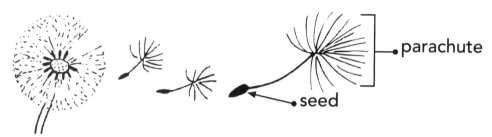

Vocabulary

conditions
things that are needed before something else can happen

parachute
the part of a dandelion that causes the seed to float in the air

A. Use the vocabulary words to complete each sentence.

1. A dandelion seed can travel away from its parent

plant because it has a _____.

2. A seed will only grow where the _____ are just right.

B. Write **true** or **false**.

1. Parachutes can grow into new dandelions. _____

2. A child blowing on a dandelion is helping
the dandelion distribute its seeds. _____

C. Do you think dandelions would grow closer together or
farther apart in places that have a lot of wind? Why?

_____

Name _____

Day 3
Weekly Question
Why do dandelions turn white and fluffy?

All seeds are covered by a **seed coat**. The seed coat protects the living part of the seed, called the **seed germ**, until it is time to grow. Seed coats protect seeds in many ways. For example, they are light and help seeds float on water. Seed coats are also hard, which protects the seed from being damaged. And some seed coats keep seeds from becoming too dry.

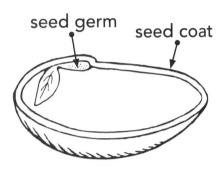

seed germ   seed coat

Vocabulary

seed coat
the outer part of a seed that is hard and protects the rest of the seed

seed germ
the part of a seed that grows into a new plant

A. Write **true** or **false**.

1. Seed coats only protect seed germs from water. _____

2. A seed germ without a seed coat would be easily damaged. _____

3. A seed coat grows into a new plant. _____

4. Seed coats keep plants from growing. _____

5. The seed germ is the part of the seed that is alive. _____

B. Suppose a dandelion seed lands on dry soil. How could the seed coat help protect the seed until rain falls?

_____

Name _____

Day 4

Weekly Question

Why do dandelions turn white and fluffy?

Dandelion seeds have special parts that allow them to be distributed by the wind. Because most seeds float, seeds can also be distributed by water. Rivers, streams, and ocean waves carry some seeds great distances.

Animals also help distribute seeds by eating them. The seed coats keep the seeds from being digested, so they pass through the animal.

Read about each kind of seed. Then write whether you think it is distributed by wind, water, or animals.

1. A coconut is the giant seed of a coconut tree. Coconuts are covered by a very hard shell, and they float.

_____

2. Barley is a plant that is similar to wheat. Its seeds have hooks that can cling to fur or clothing.

_____

3. Fruit from a blackberry plant has many tiny, hard seeds. The fruit is sweet when it is ripe. The fruit is heavy and will not scatter in the wind.

_____

4. Milkweed seeds grow in pods. They develop fluffy parachutes, similar to dandelions. The seeds are very light.

_____

Name _____

Day 5

Weekly Question

Why do dandelions turn white and fluffy?

A. Use the words in the box to complete the paragraph.

Since plants cannot move, they need to find

ways to _____ their seeds. The

seeds travel by wind, water, or animals until they

find the right _____. As seeds travel,

their _____ protects the seed germ.

conditions

distribute

seed coat

B. Label the parts of the dandelion and its seed.
Use the words in the box.

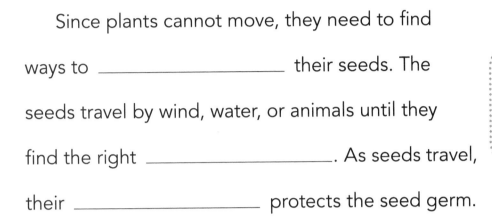

seed coat

seed germ

parachute

C. Write **wind**, **water**, or **animals** to describe the way
each seed is distributed.

_____   _____   _____

Daily Science

Big Idea 2

Plants have many parts. Each part does a special job.

Week 4

Why do leaves change color in the fall?

This week, students learn that leaves play a vital role in a plant's survival. Leaves contain the green pigment chlorophyll, which enables plants to absorb and convert the sun's energy. This process, called photosynthesis, uses sunlight to join water and carbon dioxide from the air into complex molecules that the plant uses for food. When seasons change, leaves change color. Many factors, including less sunlight and moisture in the fall, cause the production of chlorophyll to eventually stop. The green color disappears and yellows and oranges appear. These colors are always in the leaves, but they are masked by the chlorophyll until it stops production.

Day One

Vocabulary: *cell, chlorophyll*

Materials: green crayons

Distribute page 57 and introduce the vocabulary. For *cell*, you may wish to point out that all living things are made up of cells, which are too small to see without a microscope. Then have volunteers read aloud the introduction. Distribute crayons and guide students through the diagram in activity A before having them complete the page. Review students' responses together.

Day Two

Vocabulary: *carbon dioxide, photosynthesis*

Distribute page 58 and introduce the vocabulary. Say: **Carbon dioxide is a gas that is everywhere. Every time you breathe, you release carbon dioxide.** Have volunteers read the introduction aloud. Then guide students through the diagram explaining photosynthesis. Have students complete the activities and then review the answers together.

Day Three

Distribute page 59 and have volunteers read the introduction aloud. Have students complete activity A. You may want to draw a timeline on the board and have students fill in the events from the activity. Then have students complete activity B. Review students' responses together.

Day Four

Vocabulary: *conserving*

Distribute page 60 and introduce the vocabulary word. Then have volunteers read the introduction aloud. Explain that trees make more food than they need during the spring and summer, which helps them survive during the cold winter months. Say: **Most farmers are afraid of the temperature dropping suddenly during spring. Why do you think they are afraid of this?** (A freeze during spring hurts plants that are trying to grow new leaves.) Then have students complete the activities. Review the answers together.

Day Five

Tell students they will review everything they have learned about leaves. Have them complete page 61. Go over the answers together.

Name _____

Day 1

Weekly Question
Why do leaves change color in the fall?

When you picture a leaf in your mind, what color is it? If you said "green," that's not surprising. Leaves spend most of their lives being green. The green color is from a chemical called **chlorophyll**. It is stored in the leaf's **cells**. Chlorophyll absorbs sunlight and uses that energy to make food for the plant.

A. Look at the diagram of the leaf. Color it green. Then complete the caption below.

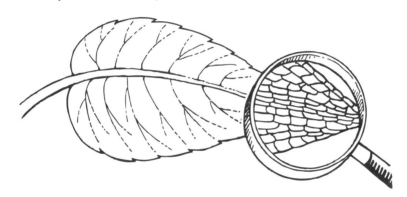

Chlorophyll makes leaves look _____.

B. Answer each question.

1. Where is chlorophyll stored in a leaf? _____

2. What two things do leaves need to make food?

_____ and _____

3. How would you be able to tell if a leaf did NOT have chlorophyll?

_____

Vocabulary

cell
the smallest unit of a plant

chlorophyll
a green chemical in plants that absorbs sunlight

Name _____

Weekly Question

Day 2

Why do leaves change color in the fall?

Chlorophyll helps plants make food through a process called **photosynthesis**. During photosynthesis, chlorophyll absorbs sunlight. This gives the plant cells energy. The plant cells use the energy to combine **carbon dioxide**, a gas in the air, with water. This becomes food for the plant.

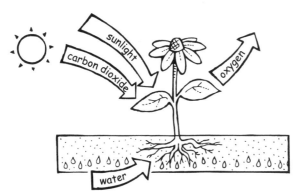

Vocabulary

carbon dioxide
a gas found in the air

photosynthesis
the process by which plants use sunlight to make their own food from carbon dioxide and water

A. Use the words in the box to complete the sentences.

> carbon dioxide   water
> photosynthesis   sunlight

1. Chlorophyll absorbs _____ during

   _____.

2. During photosynthesis, _____

   and _____ combine to make food.

B. Summer days are the longest of the year and have the most sunlight. Winter days are the shortest and have the least amount of sunlight. When do you think plants make the most food?

_____

Name _____

Day 3

Weekly Question

Why do leaves change color in the fall?

In the fall, days become shorter. There is less sunlight. The approach of winter brings colder temperatures, and there is less water in the air. With less water and less sunlight, photosynthesis slows down. Leaves stop making chlorophyll, so they stop making food. When the green chlorophyll disappears, other colors such as yellow and orange appear in the leaves. These colors were always there. They were just covered up by the chlorophyll.

A. Number the events below in the correct order.

_____ Days are shorter and there is less sunlight.

_____ Summer turns to fall.

_____ Photosynthesis slows down.

_____ Leaves change color.

_____ Leaves stop making food and chlorophyll.

B. Some trees that change color in the fall in the north will stay green all year in the south. Why do you think this happens?

_____

Day 4

Weekly Question

Why do leaves change color in the fall?

As soon as leaves stop making chlorophyll, they change color, die, and fall from the tree. But the tree is not dead. The tree is **conserving** energy. It lives on the extra food it made during the summer.

In spring, the days grow longer. It is warmer, and there is more water in the air. New leaves grow. They start producing chlorophyll. The plant begins to make food again.

Vocabulary

conserving
saving or storing

A. Write **true** or **false**.

1. A runner in a race would conserve energy by slowing down.

_____

2. Warmer temperatures and more sunlight signal trees to make chlorophyll again.

_____

B. List three changes that happen in the spring that tell a plant it is time to grow new leaves.

1. _____

2. _____

3. _____

C. New leaves in spring sometimes look light green or yellowish-green, but turn darker green by summer. What do you suppose is happening?

_____

Name ________________________________

Day 5

Weekly Question

Why do leaves change color in the fall?

Daily Science **Big Idea 2** **WEEK 4**

A. Use the words in the box to complete each sentence.

chlorophyll	**carbon dioxide**	**photosynthesis**

1. Most plants make their own food through the process of ____________________.
2. Leaves use ____________________ from the air to make food.
3. All green leaves contain ____________________.

B. Write **true** or **false**.

1. When there is less sunlight, leaves produce more food. __________
2. When chlorophyll is gone, other colors such as yellow appear. __________
3. Trees make only enough food for the summer. __________
4. In winter, leaves and trees both die. __________

C. Why are leaves green in the summer?

____

Name _____

 Unit Review

Comprehension
Show What You Know

Daily Science
Big Idea 2
WEEK 5

Read each item. Fill in the bubble next to the correct answer.

1. In a plant, water travels from the _____.

Ⓐ roots to the leaves   Ⓒ stem to the roots

Ⓑ leaves to the ground   Ⓓ roots to the soil

2. Leaves change color because _____.

Ⓐ they release water   Ⓒ they produce food

Ⓑ chlorophyll turns yellow   Ⓓ chlorophyll is gone

3. All of the following are fruits except _____.

Ⓐ tomatoes   Ⓒ watermelons

Ⓑ carrots   Ⓓ cherries

4. Seeds floating on water or air are examples of how plants _____.

Ⓐ make food   Ⓒ make seeds

Ⓑ distribute seeds   Ⓓ get water

5. What must all plants have to survive?

Ⓐ sunlight   Ⓒ nutrients

Ⓑ water   Ⓓ all of these

6. How does chlorophyll help plants?

Ⓐ It absorbs sunlight.   Ⓒ It distributes seeds.

Ⓑ It moves water.   Ⓓ It protects the plant.

Name _____

Unit Review

Vocabulary

Word Matching

A. Match each word with its meaning.

1. chlorophyll •   • the smallest unit of a plant

2. fruit   •   • tiny holes in leaves that open and close

3. vegetable   •   • the part of a plant that contains seeds

4. cell   •   • a green chemical that absorbs sunlight

5. seed coat   •   • a stem, leaf, or root that you can eat

6. pores   •   • to scatter

7. nutrients   •   • a covering that protects the seed germ

8. distribute   •   • substances in soil necessary for healthy plants

B. Use the words in the box to complete each sentence.

> **parachute   photosynthesis   pollen**

1. A flower needs _____ in order to make seeds.

2. The process by which plants make their own food is

   called _____.

3. A _____ helps plants use the wind to
   distribute seeds.

Name _____

Unit Review

Visual Literacy

Burrs and Fur

Some plants make seeds that have little hooks. These hooks can attach to animals passing by. Barley is a type of grass that distributes its seeds this way.

Look at each picture below. Then write the letter of the caption that matches that picture.

How Barley Distributes Its Seeds

_____

_____

_____

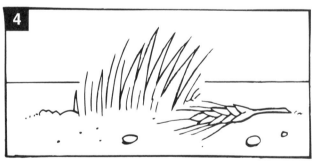

_____

a. The dog scratches and sheds the seeds.

b. The dog rubs against the grass.

c. Seeds land on the ground and later grow into new plants.

d. Barley seeds attach themselves to the dog's fur.

Name _____

Unit Review

Hands-on Activity

Color a Carnation

Here's how to create different-colored flowers by using a plant's ability to absorb water through its stem.

What You Need

- white carnations
- several vases or tall plastic cups
- water
- food coloring
- scissors

1. Fill each vase halfway with water.

2. Put 10 to 20 drops of food coloring in each vase. Use a different color for each vase.

3. Ask an adult to help you cut the flower stems an inch from the bottom.

4. Put one or two flowers in each vase. Use all the flowers.

5. Leave the flowers in the water overnight.

What Did You Discover?

1. What happened to the flowers after they sat in the water overnight?

   _____

2. What does this activity show about how water moves through a plant?

   _____

3. What do you think would happen if you split the stem so that half was in one color of water and half was in another color of water?

   _____

Big Idea 3

Fossils tell us about the plants and animals that lived long ago.

Key Concepts
Fossils, Earth's Formation

National Standard
Fossils provide evidence about the plants and animals that lived long ago and the nature of the environment at that time.

Most third-grade students know something about dinosaurs and other early life-forms on Earth. However, students may not yet have learned how scientists investigate extinct animals. Fossils play an important role as scientists "dig" for information about Earth's past. This Big Idea teaches students that:

→ fossils are formed in different ways;

→ many fossils can be found in sedimentary rocks;

→ scientists can determine the age of fossils from the sedimentary layers in which they are found; and

→ the movements of the Earth's layers sometimes cause ocean fossils to end up on mountains.

Teacher Background

Through studying geologic layers and fossils, scientists have learned about animals and plants that became extinct millions of years ago.

The uncovering of fossil evidence is a continuing detective story. From footprints to leaves, bones, and other fragments, scientists have been able to reconstruct Earth's past by using the fossil record.

Fossils have been found on every continent, but only a small portion of life on Earth has been preserved in the fossil record. This fascinating evidence trapped in the rocks of Earth's crust also provides clues as to how the Earth's crust has moved and changed. In this unit, students will learn about the value of fossils and their role in scientific discovery.

For specific background information on each week's concepts, refer to the notes on pp. 68, 74, 80, and 86.

Unit Overview

WEEK 1: How does something become a fossil?

Connection to the Big Idea: Students learn what fossils are and how they are formed. They then learn about the different kinds of fossils: cast, mold, and trace.

Content Vocabulary: *amber, cast, decay, fossil, minerals, mold, resin, sediment, trace fossil*

WEEK 2: Where is the best place to look for fossils?

Connection to the Big Idea: Students learn that all fossils are found in sedimentary rock. They also learn that paleontologists find fossils as rock erodes or when people dig. Students discover that different types of rock have different fossils and that, while fossils are found everywhere on Earth, some places have more fossils than other places.

Content Vocabulary: *erodes, paleontologist, preserve, sedimentary rock*

WEEK 3: How do scientists know how old a fossil is?

Connection to the Big Idea: Students learn that scientists use fossils to determine Earth's age. Students discover that Earth's history is divided into blocks of time and that scientists use marker fossils to learn when certain animals or plants lived and became extinct.

Content Vocabulary: *fossil record, marker fossil, trilobite*

WEEK 4: Why are fossils of ocean animals found on mountains today?

Connection to the Big Idea: Students first learn about Earth's layers and how Earth's crust is always moving, which creates faults and causes continents to push against one another. Students also learn that this movement can cause the sea floor to rise and mountains to form, explaining how fossils of sea animals can end up in mountains millions of years later.

Content Vocabulary: *collide, continents, crust, faults, lava, mantle*

WEEK 5: Unit Review

You may choose to do these activities to review concepts about fossils.

p. 92: Comprehension Students answer multiple-choice questions about important concepts from the unit.

p. 93: Vocabulary Students use key vocabulary from the unit to answer either/or questions.

p. 94: Visual Literacy Students match captions to illustrations about fossils in the La Brea Tar Pits in California.

p. 95: Hands-on Activity Students make a mold fossil from plaster of Paris. Instructions and materials needed for the activity are listed on the student page.

Daily Science

Big Idea 3

Fossils tell us about the plants and animals that lived long ago.

Week 1

How does something become a fossil?

Students learn that fossils are the remains of living things from millions of years ago. The word *fossil* comes from the Latin word "to dig up." Fossils are formed when a plant or an animal is quickly covered by sediment after death. Living things with hard remains, such as bones, shells, or wood, can become cast fossils. Remains that decay away entirely can leave their imprint behind on rocks. These are mold fossils. Another type of fossil comes from amber, which is fossilized tree resin. And there are also trace fossils, which are fossils of animal activity, such as burrows, footprints, and droppings.

Day One

Vocabulary: *decay, fossil, sediment*

Materials: modeling clay, small objects such as buttons and paper clips

Distribute page 69 and introduce the vocabulary words. Then have volunteers read the introduction aloud. Demonstrate how fossils form by covering several small objects with the modeling clay. Say: **Imagine that the modeling clay is sediment and these objects are the remains of plants and animals.** Have students surmise how the sediment protects the remains. (It protects them from weathering, other animals, etc.) Have students complete the activities, and then review the answers together.

Day Two

Vocabulary: *cast, minerals*

Materials: plastic building blocks, modeling clay

Distribute page 70 and introduce the vocabulary. Then have volunteers read the introduction aloud. Use the plastic building blocks to explain how casts are made. Arrange the blocks to make a basic shape and say: **Imagine that the blocks are a bone and the clay is minerals.** Remove one of the blocks and replace it with some modeling clay. Say: **As the original bone decays, minerals take its place.** Have students complete the activities. For the last question, remind students that worms have no hard parts.

Day Three

Vocabulary: *mold, trace fossil*

Distribute page 71 and introduce the vocabulary. Have volunteers read the introduction aloud. Then direct students to complete the activities. For the last question, remind students what a cast fossil is. Consider giving students a hint by reminding them that only hard things can become casts, while both hard and soft things can become molds.

Day Four

Vocabulary: *amber, resin*

Materials: amber or resin (optional)

Distribute page 72 and introduce the vocabulary. Have volunteers read the introduction aloud. Show students the amber or resin if you have them. Direct students to complete the activities. For the last question, refer students to the picture of the insect trapped in amber. Then review the answers together.

Day Five

Tell students they will review what they have learned about how fossils are made. Have them complete page 73. Go over the answers together.

Daily Science • EMC 5013 • © Evan-Moor Corp.

Name _____

Day 1

Weekly Question

How does something become a fossil?

A **fossil** is the remains or traces of a plant or an animal that lived long ago. Fossils form when living things die and get buried quickly, before their bones, shells, or other hard parts **decay**. Usually this happens when an animal or a plant falls into water and is covered quickly by **sediment**. Floods, volcanic eruptions, or sandstorms can also bury plants and animals quickly. However, it takes thousands or even millions of years for the buried remains to become fossils.

A. Look at the diagram below. Label the **fossil** and the **sediment**.

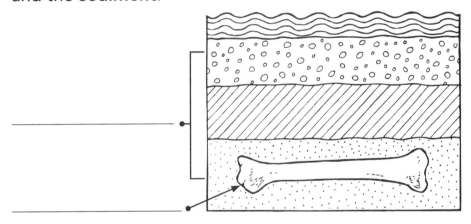

Vocabulary

decay
to rot or break down

fossil
the hardened remains or traces of an animal or a plant from long ago

sediment
soil or sand that settles to the bottom of a river, lake, or ocean

B. Write **true** or **false**.

1. An animal or a plant decays only if it has been buried.   _____

2. Sand and soil are two kinds of sediment.   _____

3. A dead plant will turn into a fossil within ten years.   _____

Name _____

When living things die, they are buried by sediment. Water, which contains **minerals**, seeps into the remains. Over many years, as more layers of sediment pile up, the weight causes the sediment to harden into rock. These hardened minerals create fossils.

Most fossils are formed when minerals replace the hard parts of a plant or an animal, such as wood or bones. This is called a **cast**.

Vocabulary

cast
a fossil made when minerals take the place of hard plant or animal parts

minerals
things found in nature that are not animal or plant

A. Which one of these is a cast? Circle it.

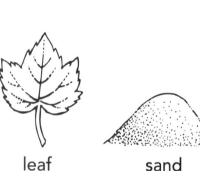
leaf

sand

dinosaur bone

snail

B. Answer each question.

1. What replaces the hard parts in plants and animals to create casts? _____

2. What do layers of sediment harden into over time? _____

3. Would a worm make a cast? Why or why not?

_____

Name _____

Day 3

Weekly Question

How does something become a fossil?

Sometimes a plant or an animal decays entirely after being buried in sediment. It leaves only its shape in the rock. This kind of fossil is called a **mold**.

Another kind of fossil is a **trace fossil**. This fossil isn't from the remains of a plant or an animal. It is from signs of animal activity. Footprints, nests, and droppings are examples of trace fossils. They help scientists learn about how the animals behaved or moved.

Vocabulary

mold
a fossil made when an animal or a plant rots away, leaving its shape in the rock

trace fossil
a fossil of an animal's footprints, droppings, or other signs of activity

A. Which of these would NOT make a trace fossil? Check the boxes next to the correct answers.

☐ a leaf   ☐ a footprint   ☐ a tooth   ☐ a nest

B. Answer the questions.

1. Why are trace fossils important to scientists?

_____

2. Do you think it is more common to find a **cast** or a **mold**? Explain.

_____

_____

Name _____

Day 4

Weekly Question

How does something become a fossil?

Imagine that it is 90 million years ago. A soft, sticky liquid called **resin** drips from a tree. A tiny insect lands on the tree trunk and becomes trapped in the resin. The insect dies, and more resin covers it so that the insect doesn't decay. Eventually the tree dies, falls into a swamp, and is covered by sediment. Millions of years pass. The resin has turned into a clear yellow fossil called **amber**. The tiny insect can still be seen inside!

A. Number the pictures to show the order in which an amber fossil forms.

 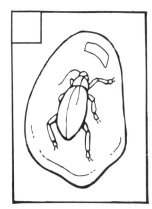 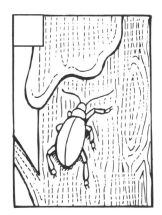

Vocabulary

amber
a yellow or brownish-yellow fossil made from tree resin

resin
a soft, thick, sticky substance that flows from some trees

B. Write a vocabulary word to complete each sentence.

1. Resin pressed in sediment becomes _____.

2. Insects trapped in _____ may become fossils millions of years from now.

C. What is one thing an amber fossil can tell scientists that a trace fossil cannot?

_____

Name _____

Day 5

Weekly Question

How does something become a fossil?

A. Name each kind of fossil. Use the words in the box.

amber   cast   trace   mold

_____   _____   _____   _____

B. Write **true** or **false**.

1. Fossils form quickly and are very common.   _____

2. Minerals take the place of bones in cast fossils.   _____

3. A flower can leave a mold fossil.   _____

C. Order the steps below to show how mold fossils are made.

____   The remains decay and leave their shape in the rock.

____   A plant or an animal dies and is quickly covered by sediment.

____   Layers of sediment build up and become hard.

Fossils tell us about the plants and animals that lived long ago.

Week 2

Where is the best place to look for fossils?

Students learn that all fossils are found in sedimentary rocks, the most common type of rock found on Earth's surface. Fossils have been found on every continent, usually when rock is removed and exposes the fossil. This can happen naturally—through erosion, earthquakes, or weathering—or when people dig. Students will also learn about some different kinds of sedimentary rock (sandstone, limestone, and shale) and about different places on Earth that are good fossil sites.

Day One

Vocabulary: *preserve, sedimentary rock*

Materials: samples or pictures of sedimentary rock

Distribute page 75 and introduce the vocabulary. Remind students that one kind of sediment is sand. Ask: **Do you think that some kinds of sedimentary rock are made from sand?** (yes) Have volunteers read the introduction aloud. Show students pictures or samples of sedimentary rock. Be sure to point out the layers. Then have students answer the questions. Review the answers together.

Day Two

Vocabulary: *erodes, paleontologist*

Distribute page 76 and introduce the vocabulary. Have volunteers read the introduction aloud. Point out the pictures in activity A. Discuss some places where erosion occurs. (coastlines, riverbeds, etc.) Then invite students to guess where people dig and find fossils. (when building new buildings, farming, etc.) Have students complete the activities. Then review the answers together.

Day Three

Materials: samples or pictures of limestone, sandstone, and shale (optional)

Distribute page 77. Have volunteers read the introduction aloud. If you brought in samples or pictures of the different types of rocks, allow students to examine them. Then guide students through the chart. Explain that sea lilies are a type of ocean plant and that mollusks are underwater animals, such as clams and snails. Then have students answer the questions. Have volunteers share their answers for the last question.

Day Four

Distribute page 78. Have volunteers read the introduction aloud. Explain that some places on Earth experienced major events, such as massive floods, mudslides, or volcanic eruptions. Say: **These places became good locations for fossils because so many living things were buried so quickly.** Guide students through the chart and timeline before they complete the activities. Then review the answers together.

Day Five

Tell students they will review everything they have learned about fossils. Have students complete page 79. Go over the answers together.

Name _____

Day 1

Weekly Question

Where is the best place to look for fossils?

Rock made from sediment is called **sedimentary rock**. As layers of sediment build up over millions of years, the top layers press down on the bottom layers. This pressure turns the layers into rock. Sandstone, limestone, and shale are all types of sedimentary rock.

Sedimentary rocks contain many fossils because the remains of plants and animals become trapped in layers of sediment. As new layers of sediment are added, these layers protect and **preserve** the covered remains.

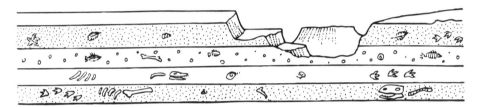

Write the answer to each question.

1. What are two kinds of sedimentary rock?

_____   _____

2. What happens to the bottom layers of sediment as new layers are added?

_____

3. Granite is a kind of rock that is formed by the cooling of very hot, melted rock inside Earth. Why wouldn't you expect to find fossils in granite?

_____

_____

Vocabulary

preserve
to protect from damage and keep in a certain condition

sedimentary rock
a type of rock formed from layers of sediment

Name _____

Day 2 | *Weekly Question*
Where is the best place to look for fossils?

Fossils are on every continent. They are actually easy to find because most of the rock we see is sedimentary rock. We find fossils when we dig up the rock or when the rock **erodes** and reveals buried layers.

Scientists who study fossils are called **paleontologists**. When paleontologists find a fossil that they want to study, they use special tools to remove the layers of sedimentary rock from around the fossil. The paleontologists must be careful because fossils can be damaged easily.

Vocabulary

erodes
wears away

paleontologist
a scientist who studies fossils

A. Circle the fossil in each picture. Write whether the picture shows **eroding** or **digging** to tell how the fossil was revealed.

_____   _____

B. Write **true** or **false**.

1. Fossils can be damaged easily. _____

2. Fossils are found in only some parts of the world. _____

3. A paleontologist mainly studies how rocks erode. _____

Name _____

Day 3

Weekly Question

Where is the best place to look for fossils?

To find fossils, paleontologists have to know a lot about rocks. They have to know how and when different kinds of sedimentary rocks formed so they know where to look for certain kinds of fossils. Paleontologists also study rocks to find out what the weather was like millions of years ago. Sometimes, paleontologists find ripples from waves and holes from raindrops made millions of years ago!

Read the chart. Then use it to help you answer the questions.

	Rock	Formed By...	Types of Fossils
	Sandstone	wind, water, ice	small shells, ripples
	Limestone	deep water	worms, sea lilies, mollusk shells
	Shale	mud, warm seas	animals, mud cracks, raindrops

1. What type of rock would probably have fossils of animals that lived in cold places? _____

2. What kinds of fossils would you find in limestone?

_____

3. What type of rock would help someone study the amount of rainfall long ago? _____

Weekly Question

Day 4

Where is the best place to look for fossils?

Daily Science

Big Idea 3

WEEK 2

Even though fossils exist everywhere, some places have many fossils clustered together. One place is called Burgess Shale. It is in Canada. Burgess Shale has fossils that are over 500 million years old. A lot of these are fossils of early marine animals.

A. The chart below tells about some other good places to find fossils. The timeline shows when animals at each site could have lived. Write the name of each site in the correct place above the timeline.

Site	Location	Types of Fossils
Pipe Creek Sinkhole	Swayzee, Indiana	early kinds of bears, fish, rodents, and a kind of rhinoceros
Dinosaur Cove	Victoria, Australia	dinosaurs, including one kind that probably lived in cold places
Falls of the Ohio Park	Clarksville, Indiana	marine animals, including early reptiles

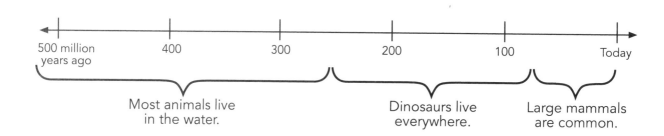

500 million years ago | 400 | 300 | 200 | 100 | Today

Most animals live in the water.

Dinosaurs live everywhere.

Large mammals are common.

B. Write **true** or **false**. Use the chart and timeline to help you.

1. The oldest fossils are found in Dinosaur Cove. _____

2. Dinosaurs are older than mammals. _____

3. Pipe Creek Sinkhole has the youngest fossils. _____

Name _____

Day 5

Weekly Question

Where is the best place to look for fossils?

A. Use the words in the box to complete the paragraph.

> erode   fossil   preserve
>
> paleontologists   sediment

A _____ is the remains of a plant or an animal from

long ago. Over millions of years, layers of _____ built

up over these remains. The layers helped _____ the

remains. Scientists called _____ study remains like

these after the rocks _____ and expose them.

B. Name two kinds of sedimentary rock where fossils can be found.

1. _____   **2.** _____

C. Write **true** or **false**.

1. Sedimentary rocks do not have layers.   _____

2. Some places have more fossils than other places.   _____

3. Fossils cannot be made in the ocean.   _____

4. Fossils of mammals are the oldest fossils.   _____

Fossils tell us about the plants and animals that lived long ago.

Week 3

How do scientists know how old a fossil is?

Students learn that the age of a fossil is determined by the layer of rock it is in. The layers above and below a rock help establish its relative age. Marker fossils are found in large numbers in certain layers. Scientists use marker fossils to determine the age of other kinds of fossils. Scientists know when dinosaurs became extinct because their fossils do not appear beyond a certain point in the fossil record.

Day One

Vocabulary: *fossil record*

Distribute page 81 and introduce the vocabulary word. Discuss different types of records that people keep. (e.g., medical records, reading records, scrapbooks, journals, etc.) Then say: **The fossil record is like nature's scrapbook—it shows us what has lived when and where on Earth.** Have volunteers read the introduction aloud. Then have students complete the activity. Review the answers together.

Day Two

Explain geological time by reviewing that Earth is billions of years old. This is such a large number that scientists have divided the time into smaller blocks, or periods, of time. Distribute page 82 and have volunteers read the introduction aloud. Guide students through the timeline on the page before having them complete the activity. For the oral activity, pair students or discuss as a group.

Day Three

Vocabulary: *marker fossil, trilobite*

Materials: sample or picture of a trilobite (optional)

Distribute page 83, introduce the vocabulary, and show students the trilobite fossil or picture if you have it. Then have volunteers read the introduction aloud. Ask students to think of plants or animals that live in great numbers on Earth today, such as ants, flies, grass, worms, etc. Say: **Some things that lived millions of years ago, such as trilobites, were just as common then as flies are today. Since there were so many of them, they had the best chance of becoming fossils. This makes them fairly common and easy to find, which is one reason scientists use them as marker fossils.** Then have students complete the activities.

Day Four

Distribute page 84 and have volunteers read the introduction aloud. Say: **Scientists work together to add to the fossil record. Whenever a scientist discovers a new fossil or new things about other kinds of fossils, the fossil record—and our understanding of Earth's history—becomes a little bit clearer.** Have students complete the activities.

Day Five

Tell students they will review everything they have learned about the ages of fossils. Have them complete page 85. Review the answers together.

Name _____

Day 1

Weekly Question

How do scientists know how old a fossil is?

Do you know how old Earth is? Nobody knows for sure, because no one was around then. Scientists believe life on Earth began over 4 billion years ago. The **fossil record** has helped scientists reach this conclusion. By studying fossils in different layers of rock, scientists can understand what Earth was like long ago.

Vocabulary

fossil record
layers of rock containing fossils that help tell the story of life on Earth

Use the diagram to help you answer the questions below.

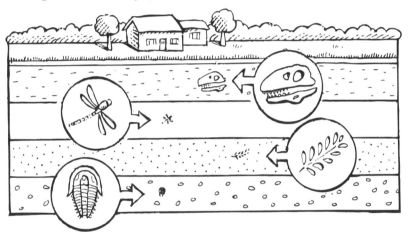

1. Are the oldest fossils in the top layer, middle layer, or bottom layer? Explain why that is.

_____

2. If scientists found a fossil in the middle layer that was 2 million years old, would they think Earth was more or less than 2 million years old? Why?

_____

3. Why are scientists interested in the fossil record?

_____

Name _____

Day 2

Weekly Question

How do scientists know how old a fossil is?

Scientists divide Earth's past into blocks of time. Each block of time, or period, is millions of years long. During each period, certain kinds of plants and animals lived. Not every plant or animal became a fossil, but enough did that scientists are able to draw conclusions about what lived during which period. The timeline below shows some of the periods in Earth's history.

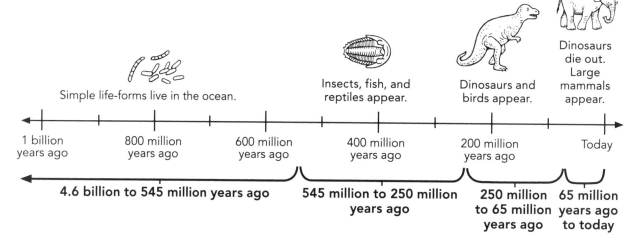

Simple life-forms live in the ocean.

Insects, fish, and reptiles appear.

Dinosaurs and birds appear.

Dinosaurs die out. Large mammals appear.

| 1 billion years ago | 800 million years ago | 600 million years ago | 400 million years ago | 200 million years ago | Today |

4.6 billion to 545 million years ago

545 million to 250 million years ago

250 million to 65 million years ago

65 million years ago to today

Write **true** or **false**.

1. Reptile fossils are older than bird fossils. _____

2. Humans and dinosaurs lived during the same time. _____

3. The newest fossils are from ocean creatures. _____

4. Fish appeared on Earth after mammals did. _____

 Talk

Which time period do you think scientists know more about, 500 million years ago or 65 million years ago? Why do you think that? Discuss it with your partner.

Name _____

Day 3

Weekly Question

How do scientists know how old a fossil is?

Whenever a scientist finds a new or unfamiliar fossil, he or she will look at a **marker fossil** for clues about the age of the unfamiliar fossil. For example, **trilobites** are marker fossils. These extinct insect-like sea animals were so common 250 to 520 million years ago that there are more fossils of trilobites than fossils of other creatures. So they serve as "markers" of the time period they are from. If a scientist finds a new kind of fossil in the same rock as a trilobite fossil, the scientist can figure out when the unfamiliar plant or animal lived.

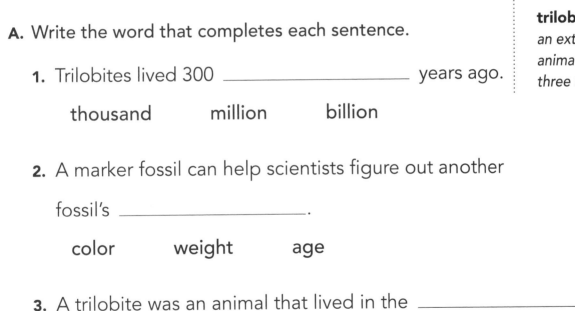

trilobite

Vocabulary

marker fossil
common fossils that help scientists learn about newer fossils

trilobite
an extinct sea animal that had three body parts

A. Write the word that completes each sentence.

1. Trilobites lived 300 _____ years ago.

   thousand   million   billion

2. A marker fossil can help scientists figure out another

   fossil's _____.

   color   weight   age

3. A trilobite was an animal that lived in the _____.

   ocean   ground   mountains

B. Since trilobites were so common in the past, they made many fossils. What creature living today might make a lot of fossils, like the trilobite did? Explain your answer.

Name _____

How do scientists know how old a fossil is?

Daily Science

Big Idea 3

WEEK 3

Scientists study the fossil record to tell when different plants and animals lived. The fossil record also tells scientists when these plants and animals disappeared. For example, many different kinds of trilobites lived on Earth, but their fossils only appear in rocks that are more than about 250 million years old. This tells us that trilobites have been extinct for about 250 million years.

Dinosaur fossils are found only in rocks that are between 65 and 130 million years old. So we know that dinosaurs disappeared from Earth around 65 million years ago.

A. Answer the questions.

1. What can scientists learn by studying the fossil record?

   _____

2. What kind of fossil could you find in a rock that is 100 million years old but not in a rock that is 50 million years old?

   _____

3. If you found a rock with a dinosaur footprint in it, would you expect to find a trilobite fossil in the same rock? Why or why not?

   _____

B. An ammonite (AM-uh-nite) was a tiny sea animal that lived between 65 million and 400 million years ago. Fill in the bar over the timeline to show when the ammonite lived.

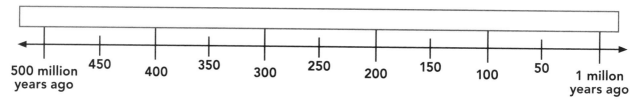

500 million years ago   450   400   350   300   250   200   150   100   50   1 million years ago

Daily Science • EMC 5013 • © Evan-Moor Corp.

Name _____

Day 5

How do scientists know how old a fossil is?

Daily Science

Big Idea 3

WEEK 3

A. Use the words in the box to complete the paragraph.

> trilobite   fossil record   marker fossil

Scientists study the _____ to learn about

the life-forms that lived on Earth long ago. For example, one type

of sea animal was the _____. This creature was so

common for millions of years that it left behind many fossils. This

makes it a good _____ for scientists to use.

B. Use the timeline to complete each sentence.

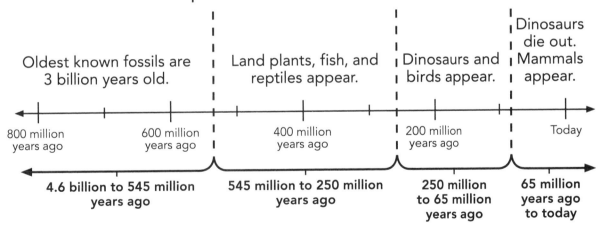

1. Dinosaurs appeared on Earth about _____ million years ago.

2. The first land plants appeared about _____ million years ago.

3. The fossil record started _____ billion years ago.

4. Large mammals appeared _____ million years ago.

Daily Science

Big Idea 3

Fossils tell us about the plants and animals that lived long ago.

Week 4

Why are fossils of ocean animals found on mountains today?

This week, students learn about why sea fossils are found in the mountains. Because Earth's surface is constantly in motion, the world looked very different hundreds of millions of years ago. The continents have been joined together several times over the past 4 billion years. As continents move together and drift apart, they create mountains and seas. Everything that is buried now travels with that continent.

Day One

Vocabulary: *crust, lava*

Materials: dough made from 1 cup flour, 1/2 cup salt, and 1 cup water

Prior to class, mix the dough and form a large ball. Place it in a well-ventilated area, as you want it to begin to dry and crack on the outside, while the center remains soft. Distribute page 87 and introduce the vocabulary. Have volunteers read aloud the introduction. Point out the picture and say: **Earth was a very different place 4 billion years ago. There were no plants or animals. Our planet was brand new.** Show students the ball of drying dough and let them examine it. Explain how Earth's crust cooled but the inside was still soft, like the ball of dough. Then have students complete the activities.

Day Two

Vocabulary: *faults, mantle*

Distribute page 88 and introduce the vocabulary. Have volunteers read the introduction aloud. Then point out the diagram and explain how Earth is divided into layers. Explain that the core is mostly liquid iron and is extremely hot. Have students complete the activity. For the oral activity, pair students or discuss the question as a class.

Day Three

Vocabulary: *collide, continents*

Distribute page 89 and introduce the vocabulary. Challenge students to name the seven continents. (Africa, Antarctica, Asia, Australia, Europe, North and South America) Then have volunteers read the introduction aloud. Guide students through the pictures in activity A. Have students number the sentences. Then have students complete activity B. Review the answers together.

Day Four

Distribute page 90. Have volunteers read aloud the introduction. Guide students through the maps in activity A and reiterate that Earth's continents are always moving. Explain that scientists believe that one day, millions of years from now, the continents will come back together again. Distribute crayons and point out what happened to Europe, Asia, and India in the two maps. Then have students complete the activities.

Day Five

Tell students they will review what they have learned about how mountains form. Have them complete page 91. Go over the answers together.

Daily Science • EMC 5013 • © Evan-Moor Corp.

Name _____

Day 1

Weekly Question

Why are fossils of ocean animals found on mountains today?

To understand how fossils can end up in different places on Earth, first we have to understand more about Earth. Earth hasn't always looked like it does today. When Earth first formed over 4 billion years ago, it was very hot and covered in **lava**. As Earth cooled, the lava cooled, too, and formed the land on Earth's **crust**. Steam escaped from underneath Earth's crust and turned into water. This formed the oceans.

Vocabulary

crust
Earth's outer layer of rock and water

lava
very hot liquid rock

A. Number the sentences to show the correct order of events.

____ Oceans were formed.   ____ Land was formed.

____ All the lava cooled.   ____ Steam escaped from the crust.

B. Answer the questions.

1. How was Earth different 4 billion years ago from today?

_____

2. The oldest fossils are of things that lived in the ocean. What does this tell you about where life probably formed on Earth?

_____

Name _____

Day 2

Weekly Question

Why are fossils of ocean animals found on mountains today?

The ground beneath our feet is on the move! This movement is very slow, so we don't usually feel it unless we live along giant **faults**. People near faults feel the ground move during earthquakes. But scientists know that Earth's crust has always been moving. The crust is actually just a small part of the planet. Beneath the crust, Earth's hot, softer **mantle** moves, too. During the past 4 billion years, Earth's surface has moved a lot. That means any fossils buried in the crust at different times have also moved.

Vocabulary

faults
deep cracks in Earth's crust

mantle
the hot, softer rock beneath Earth's crust

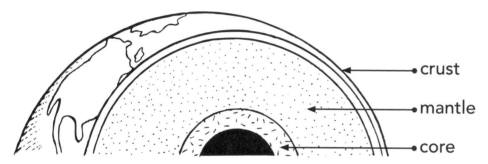

Write **crust** or **mantle** to answer the questions.

1. Which layer of Earth do we live on?   _____

2. Which layer of Earth is hotter?   _____

3. Which layer of Earth has faults?   _____

4. Which layer of Earth is thicker?   _____

 Talk

Do you think the crust would move more or less if the mantle were cool and hard? Discuss it with your partner.

Name _____

Day 3

Weekly Question

Why are fossils of ocean animals found on mountains today?

The movement of Earth's **continents** builds mountains. When two continents **collide**, the rock layers in each continent push together and move up. Sometimes the layers are pushed up all the way from the ocean floor. If those rock layers contain fossils, the fossils travel up with the rocks.

The Himalaya (him-uh-LAY-uh) Mountains are the highest in the world. They were formed when India collided with Asia and pushed up an ancient seabed called the Tethys Sea. So now there are fossils of sea creatures at the top of the tallest mountains!

Vocabulary

collide
to run or crash into

continents
the seven largest landmasses on Earth

A. Number the sentences in the correct order to match them with the pictures.

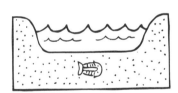
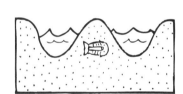
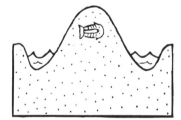

_____ The sea floor rises, taking the fossil with it.

_____ The ground rises higher, becoming a mountain.

_____ A living creature dies and is covered by sediment.

B. Write the two missing words to complete the sentence.

The Himalaya _____ were formed when

two _____ collided.

Name _____

Day 4

Weekly Question

Why are fossils of ocean animals found on mountains today?

Scientists study fossils to learn how the continents have moved over time. For example, the same type of fern fossil has been found on every continent. This means that the continents must have been connected when that kind of fern was alive 250 million years ago. This giant landmass was called Pangaea (pan-JEE-uh).

A. Look at the map of Earth today. Color each continent a different color. Then find the matching continent shapes on Pangaea. Color them the same color.

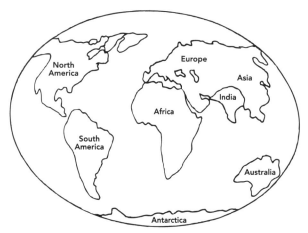

The continents today

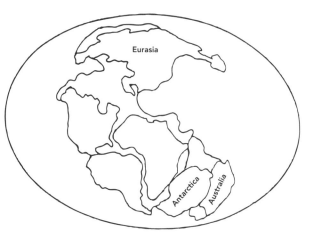

Pangaea 250 million years ago

B. Write **true** or **false**.

1. Earth has always looked the way it does now.   _____

2. South America was once next to Africa.   _____

3. Fossils can tell us what Earth looked like long ago.   _____

Name _____

Day 5 *Weekly Question*
Why are fossils of ocean animals found on mountains today?

A. Fill in the bubble next to the correct answer.

1. Where is the ground most likely to move?

   Ⓐ near a fault   Ⓒ near a city

   Ⓑ in the ocean   Ⓓ on a mountain

2. What are continents?

   Ⓐ underwater mountains   Ⓒ fossils on mountains

   Ⓑ giant landmasses   Ⓓ pieces of Earth's mantle

3. What happens when landmasses collide?

   Ⓐ They form oceans.   Ⓒ They form Earth's crust.

   Ⓑ They form fossils.   Ⓓ They form mountains.

4. What formed the land on Earth's crust?

   Ⓐ cooling lava   Ⓒ giant oceans

   Ⓑ ice comets   Ⓓ colliding continents

B. Antarctica and Australia were connected until about 250 million years ago. If you found a fossil of the same kind of animal on both continents today, how old would the fossil be? Explain your answer.

_____

_____

_____

Name _____

Unit Review

Comprehension

Fossils and Earth's History

Fill in the bubble next to the correct answer.

1. Layers of mud or sand that become hard are called _____.

   Ⓐ sedimentary rock   Ⓒ lava

   Ⓑ amber   Ⓓ fossils

2. The layer of Earth where fossils are found is the _____.

   Ⓐ mantle   Ⓒ crust

   Ⓑ core   Ⓓ mountains

3. Earth's oldest fossils are from _____.

   Ⓐ early mammals   Ⓒ dinosaurs

   Ⓑ ocean creatures   Ⓓ birds

4. Mountains are formed when _____.

   Ⓐ water erodes rock   Ⓒ fossils pile up

   Ⓑ sediment becomes rock   Ⓓ continents collide

5. Cast fossils are made of _____.

   Ⓐ leaves   Ⓒ shells

   Ⓑ minerals   Ⓓ wood

6. Trilobites are examples of _____.

   Ⓐ amber   Ⓒ sedimentary rocks

   Ⓑ marker fossils Ⓓ dinosaurs

Name _____

Unit Review

Vocabulary

Either/Or Questions

Daily Science

Big Idea 3

WEEK 5

Write each answer.

1. Is the Earth's **crust** hard or soft? _____

2. Is **amber** a fossil or a living plant? _____

3. Is a dinosaur footprint a **mollusk** or a **trace fossil**? _____

4. Is a **trilobite** a mountain or a fossil? _____

5. Is the **fossil record** in a book or in layers of rock? _____

6. Does a **paleontologist** study fossils or people? _____

7. Are **minerals** living or nonliving? _____

8. What is the middle layer of Earth called, the **crust** or the **mantle**? _____

9. If you **preserve** something, do you keep it or throw it away? _____

10. If something **decays**, does it last forever or go away? _____

Name _____

Scientists are digging up fossils even in the city of Los Angeles, California! The site is called the La Brea (lah BRAY-uh) Tar Pits. Scientists have found the bones of sabertooth cats and Columbian mammoths. These animals were trapped in the pits 30,000 years ago.

Write the letter of the caption that matches each picture.

1

_____

2

_____

3

_____

4

_____

a. A hungry sabertooth cat attacked the mammoth.

b. Over time, both animals were buried in the pit.

c. A mammoth wandered into a pool of sticky oil and sand.

d. The sabertooth cat was stuck, and died of hunger.

Name _____

Unit Review

Hands-on Activity

Make Your Own Fossil

Fossils form in a number of ways. Try making your own fossils!

What You Need

- plaster of Paris
- petroleum jelly
- water
- bowl
- leaves
- shells
- cardboard

1. Follow the directions to mix the plaster and the water. Have an adult help you.

2. Spread some plaster on the cardboard. Use enough plaster so you can press the leaf and shell into it later.

3. Coat the leaf and shell with petroleum jelly.

4. Press the leaf and shell gently into the plaster. Try not to move them once they are in the plaster.

5. Let the plaster dry overnight. When it is dry, carefully remove the leaf and the shell.

What Did You Discover?

1. What type of fossil did you make, a **mold** or a **cast** fossil?

_____

2. Why do you think scientists are very careful when they remove fossils?

_____

3. What other kinds of fossils could you make this way?

_____

Big Idea 4

Air is a gas that surrounds us, takes up space, and creates weather.

Key Concepts
Air and Weather

National Standard
Weather can be described by measurable quantities, such as temperature, wind direction, and speed.

Third-grade students have a basic understanding that wind is a weather phenomenon. But students may not be aware that there is an atmosphere around Earth and that it plays a role in creating our weather. This Big Idea teaches students:

→ what the atmosphere is made of and what it does;

→ what air pressure is;

→ how wind is created in the atmosphere; and

→ how some properties of air affect flight.

Teacher Background

Earth's atmosphere is an invisible protective layer of gases that blanket our planet. The atmosphere is made mostly of nitrogen and oxygen, which we need to breathe and survive. The atmosphere absorbs and reflects the most harmful rays of sunlight, and even causes some space rocks and debris to incinerate before reaching the surface.

Without the atmosphere, there would be no weather. The atmosphere allows winds to redistribute heat from the sun, and it is an important part of the water cycle. Scientists who study weather look at a number of different phenomena to get a more accurate picture of what our atmosphere is and how it affects us on Earth. By learning about air temperature, wind direction and speed, and the effects of high and low pressure air systems, students will begin to understand the cause-and-effect relationship between changes in the atmosphere and the resulting changes in weather that we can feel and see.

For specific background information on each week's concepts, refer to the notes on pp. 98, 104, 110, and 116.

Unit Overview

WEEK 1: Why can't you breathe in outer space?

Connection to the Big Idea: Earth's atmosphere has breathable air.

Students learn that the atmosphere is made of different gases. They learn that gas is densest at sea level and that the amount of gas decreases as you go higher in altitude. Finally, they discover that space has no breathable gas, so astronauts must wear special suits to survive.

Content Vocabulary: *altitude, atmosphere, oxygen, sea level*

WEEK 2: Why does a can of soda sometimes explode when you open it?

Connection to the Big Idea: Air pressure changes as gases expand or contract.

Students learn that soda is fizzy because of carbon dioxide in the drink. They then learn that the gas inside a can creates air pressure, which causes the gas to escape quickly when the can is opened. Students also learn about other things that work using air pressure.

Content Vocabulary: *air pressure, carbon dioxide, dissolved*

WEEK 3: Where does wind come from?

Connection to the Big Idea: Wind is the movement of air, and it affects the weather.

Students learn that wind is the circulation of air at different pressures. They learn about high and low pressure systems and study some of the tools used to measure wind. Finally, students discover how people use the power of wind to do many things.

Content Vocabulary: *anemometer, circulate, meteorologist, pressure system, wind vane*

WEEK 4: How do birds fly?

Connection to the Big Idea: Birds have adaptations that take advantage of the properties of air to help them fly.

Students first learn how a bird's wings, feathers, and bones help it fly. They then learn about the role of drag, thrust, and lift in flight. They learn that some birds use thermal currents to help them glide, and that different wing sizes help different birds fly in different ways.

Content Vocabulary: *adaptations, drag, lift, thermal current, thrust*

WEEK 5: Unit Review

You may choose to do these activities to review concepts about air.

p. 122: Comprehension Students answer multiple-choice questions about key concepts from the unit.

p. 123: Vocabulary Students use vocabulary words to complete either/or questions.

p. 124: Visual Literacy Students label parts of an airplane and then show how drag, thrust, and lift help airplanes fly.

p. 125: Hands-on Activity Students create a "mini-tornado" in a bottle using water and circulation. Instructions and materials needed for the activity are listed on the student page.

Air is a gas that surrounds us, takes up space, and creates weather.

Week 1

Why can't you breathe in outer space?

The atmosphere is made up of gases that sit in "layers" above the ground. The two most prominent gases are oxygen and nitrogen, which are necessary for life on Earth. Air molecules in the atmosphere stay close to Earth's surface because of Earth's gravitational pull. This means that there is more gas closer to Earth's surface, but at higher altitudes the air molecules begin to thin out until there is no more gas and, consequently, no more atmosphere.

The term *altitude* is often used interchangeably with *elevation*; however, *altitude* is usually used in discussions about flying or space. You may wish to also define *elevation* for students, as it is commonly used in geography.

Day One
Vocabulary:
atmosphere, oxygen

Distribute page 99 and introduce the vocabulary. Then have volunteers read the introduction aloud. Use the picture on the page to help students understand how the atmosphere surrounds Earth. Then have students complete activity A independently. For activity B, help students brainstorm ways their senses tell them the air is there.

Day Two
Vocabulary: *altitude, sea level*

Distribute page 100 and introduce the vocabulary. Consider finding your town's altitude and sharing it with students. Then have volunteers read the introduction aloud. If necessary, review the concept of *gravity*. (the force that pulls everything closer to Earth) Then have students complete the activities independently. Review the answers together.

Day Three
Materials: map or photo of Death Valley (optional)

Distribute page 101 and have volunteers read the introduction aloud. For the first activity, you may want to tell students that another word for *altitude* is *elevation*. Then guide students through the chart and have them answer the questions. For the oral activity, pair students or discuss the question as a group. Then give students the elevation of where they live or help them use a resource to find the elevation.

Day Four
Materials: photos of astronauts in space (optional)

Distribute page 102 and have volunteers read the introduction aloud. Show students photos of astronauts in space if you have them. Point out each feature of the spacesuit, and then explain that the atmosphere gives us air we can breathe, protects us from the sun's rays, and keeps the temperature in a range that is comfortable for us. After students have completed the activities, invite volunteers to share their responses to activity B.

Day Five

Tell students they will review what they have learned about the atmosphere. Have them complete page 103. Go over the answers together.

Name _____

Day 1

Weekly Question

Why can't you breathe in outer space?

Air is all around us. Although we cannot see air, we can feel it and breathe it. The air surrounding Earth is called the **atmosphere**. The atmosphere is made mostly of two gases, nitrogen and **oxygen**. Earth's gravity pulls on the gases and keeps the atmosphere close to Earth's surface. This is a good thing, since we need oxygen in order to live.

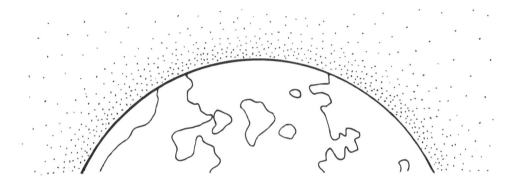

Vocabulary

atmosphere
the layers of gas that surround Earth

oxygen
a gas in the atmosphere that we breathe

A. Read each question. Fill in the bubble next to the correct answer.

1. Which of these is the atmosphere made of?

 Ⓐ solids   Ⓒ liquids

 Ⓑ gases   Ⓓ minerals

2. Which of these is true about oxygen?

 Ⓐ We can see it. Ⓒ We can breathe it.

 Ⓑ We can hold it. Ⓓ We can hear it.

B. Name two signs that tell you air is around you.

1. _____

2. _____

Name _____

Why can't you breathe in outer space?

Daily Science

Big Idea 4

WEEK 1

Earth's atmosphere is made up of many layers. Because of gravity's pull, most of the air in the atmosphere is in the bottom layer. When scientists talk about how high the atmosphere goes, they use the word **altitude**. They start measuring the altitude at **sea level**, which is the place where the land and sea are at the same level. It has an altitude of 0 feet. There is plenty of oxygen and other gases at sea level.

Vocabulary

altitude
the distance above or below sea level

sea level
where land and sea meet

A. Use the diagram below to answer the questions.

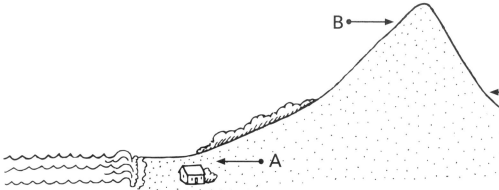

1. Where is sea level: **A**, **B**, or **C**?   _____

2. Where is the altitude the highest: **A**, **B**, or **C**?   _____

3. Is the house at a **high** or a **low** altitude?   _____

B. Write **true** or **false**.

1. The atmosphere has many layers of gas.   _____

2. Most of the air in the atmosphere is at sea level.   _____

3. **Altitude** describes how cold the atmosphere is.   _____

Name _____

Day 3

Weekly Question

Why can't you breathe in outer space?

When scientists talk about the atmosphere, they use the word **altitude** to describe how high above sea level the layers go. As the altitude increases, the atmosphere contains less gas. This means there is less oxygen to breathe. That is why it is harder to breathe at the top of a high mountain than it is to breathe at sea level.

The chart below shows the altitude of some cities in the United States. Use it to answer the questions.

City	Altitude
Denver, Colorado	5,280 feet
Flagstaff, Arizona	6,910 feet
New York, New York	768 feet
Spokane, Washington	2,376 feet

1. Which city is closest to sea level? _____

2. Which city has the highest altitude? _____

3. Would it be harder to breathe in Denver or in Flagstaff? _____

4. Is there more gas in the atmosphere in New York or in Spokane? _____

 Talk

Denver is near mountains and New York is next to the Atlantic Ocean. Think about where you live. Do you think your town has a high or a low altitude? Why? Discuss it with a partner.

Name _____

Day 4

Weekly Question

Why can't you breathe in outer space?

At about 62 miles—or over 300,000 feet above sea level—the atmosphere disappears. This is where outer space begins. Earth's gravity is too weak to pull on anything, so all the gases, including oxygen, are gone. That's why you can't breathe in outer space.

Luckily, scientists have solved that problem. Astronauts who visit space have special suits. These suits have oxygen inside of them. Wearing one of these suits is like being in your own atmosphere!

A. The diagram below shows an astronaut's suit. Draw a line to match each feature of the spacesuit to how you think it helps the astronaut.

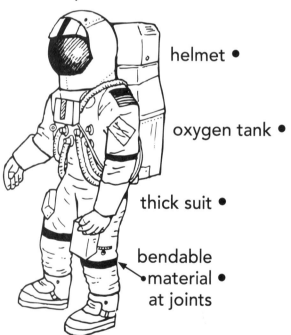

helmet •

oxygen tank •

thick suit •

• bendable material • at joints

• prevents the sun's rays from hurting the astronaut's eyes

• protects the astronaut from temperature changes in space

• allows astronauts to move and work

• holds air that astronauts can breathe

B. Explain in your own words why we can't breathe in outer space.

_____

_____

Name _____

Day 5

Weekly Question

Why can't you breathe in outer space?

A. Use the words in the box to complete the sentences.

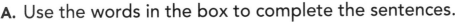

| atmosphere | altitude | oxygen | sea level |

1. The gas we breathe is called _____.

2. At _____, there is more gas in the atmosphere.

3. The _____ includes the air we breathe.

4. As the _____ goes up, the amount of gas in the atmosphere goes down.

B. Write **true** or **false**.

1. There is a lot of oxygen in outer space.   _____

2. Earth's atmosphere has only one layer.   _____

3. It is harder to breathe in the mountains than at the beach.   _____

4. Gravity keeps the air closest to Earth's surface at sea level.   _____

C. Miami, Florida, is right next to the Atlantic Ocean. Salt Lake City, Utah, is in the mountains. How do you think the atmosphere in Miami compares to the atmosphere in Salt Lake City? Write your answer.

_____

_____

Daily Science

Big Idea 4

Air is a gas that surrounds us, takes up space, and creates weather.

Week 2

Why does a can of soda sometimes explode when you open it?

Learning about why soda cans sometimes explode is relevant in a unit about weather because it is a tangible and relatable introduction to air pressure, which is a key component to wind formation and the high and low pressure systems that are responsible for weather. Air, like many other things, works to reach a state of equilibrium. An exploding soda can is evidence of the carbon dioxide that is dissolved in the soda escaping quickly to join the other gases outside the can. The same forces of air pressure at work in a can of soda are at work in the atmosphere, but on a much larger scale.

Day One Vocabulary: *carbon dioxide, dissolved*	Build background knowledge by challenging students to name the ingredients in soda. (water, carbon dioxide, sugar, flavoring) Distribute page 105 and introduce the vocabulary. Then have volunteers read the introduction aloud. Have students complete the activities.
Day Two Vocabulary: *air pressure*	Distribute page 106 and introduce the vocabulary word. Explain that air pressure comes from air "pushing" against things, but we usually don't notice this push because it isn't very strong, and because we are used to it. Have volunteers read the introduction aloud. Then have students complete the activities. Review the answers together.
Day Three Materials: a balloon	Distribute page 107. Then inflate the balloon and ask students if the air pressure inside the balloon increased or decreased. (increased) Have volunteers read the introduction aloud. If you choose, release the balloon to demonstrate how air quickly rushes out, and invite students to draw comparisons between the balloon and a can of soda. Have students complete activities A and B independently. For the oral activity, pair students or discuss the question as a group.
Day Four	Activate prior knowledge by asking students if they can think of beneficial uses for air pressure. After eliciting responses, distribute page 108 and have volunteers read the introduction aloud. Then have students complete the activities. For activity B, invite volunteers to share their drawings and describe their inventions.
Day Five	Tell students they will review what they have learned about air pressure. Have them complete page 109. Go over the answers together.

Name _____

Day 1

Weekly Question

Why does a can of soda sometimes explode when you open it?

Have you ever wondered why soda is fizzy? The two most important ingredients in soda are water and **carbon dioxide**. Carbon dioxide is a gas in the air. It is special because it can be **dissolved**, or completely mixed, into water. When carbon dioxide is mixed with water, some of it dissolves and some of it stays in the form of bubbles. The gas causes that hiss you hear when you open the can. The hiss is carbon dioxide escaping from the can.

Vocabulary

carbon dioxide
a gas in soda that makes it fizzy

dissolved
mixed completely into something

A. Write the word or phrase that completes each sentence.

1. The bubbles in soda are caused by _____.

    oxygen   carbon dioxide   soap

2. Carbon dioxide _____ when it is added to water.

    changes color   freezes   dissolves

B. Answer the questions.

1. What are the two most important ingredients in soda?

    _____ and _____

2. Why does a can of soda hiss when you open it?

    _____

Name _____

Day 2

Weekly Question

Why does a can of soda sometimes explode when you open it?

Compared to most other kinds of matter, the air in the atmosphere doesn't weigh much. Even so, there is so much air that it pushes down on everything. We call this push **air pressure**. Air pressure is the strongest at sea level. As you go higher in the atmosphere, the air pressure lessens.

We can create air pressure by forcing air into things, such as soda cans or balloons. When you blow up a balloon, you force air inside it. Dissolving carbon dioxide into soda also creates pressure inside the can.

(diagram of balloon labeled AIR PRESSURE)

Vocabulary

air pressure
the force, or push, of air

A. Look at the diagram. Complete the labels to tell where the air pressure is **highest** and where it is **lowest**.

_ _
_ ←—————— air pressure
_ _
_ ←—————— air pressure

B. Answer each question.

1. If you put air into a tire, will the pressure in the tire go up or down?

_____

2. Is air pressure stronger inside a full can of soda or an empty one?

_____

Name _____

Weekly Question

Day 3

Why does a can of soda sometimes explode when you open it?

Opening a can of soda is like releasing the air from a full balloon. The air comes out quickly and strongly until the pressure inside the balloon is the same as the pressure outside. Air spreads out so there are equal amounts of air molecules everywhere. That's why a soda sometimes explodes when you open it. Gas rushes out, and any liquid in its way is forced out, too. This can cause a huge spray!

A. Look at the pictures. Check the box next to the phrase that completes the sentence.

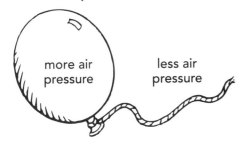

more air pressure   less air pressure

same air pressure   same air pressure

When air pressure inside the balloon goes down, _____.

☐ the balloon gets bigger   ☐ the balloon gets smaller

B. Write **true** or **false**.

1. When you open a can of soda, air pressure inside the can stays the same.   _____

2. Air molecules try to spread out evenly.   _____

Talk

When you leave a can of soda open overnight, the soda becomes "flat." Why do you think that happens? Discuss it with a partner.

Name _____

Day 4

Weekly Question

Why does a can of soda sometimes explode when you open it?

We use air pressure in many different ways. The tires on a bike are full of air. This helps the bike move easily over the road. Divers use tanks full of air to breathe underwater. Cleaning products and even some foods come in cans that have lots of air pressure, too. The pressure inside makes whatever is inside the can spray out when you press a button.

A. Name two things you have seen or used that work because of air pressure.

1. _____   2. _____

B. Work with a partner to invent a machine that uses air pressure to do a job. Draw a picture of it, and then describe how it works and what it does.

_____

_____

Name _____

Day 5

Weekly Question

Why does a can of soda sometimes explode when you open it?

A. Use the words in the box to complete each sentence.

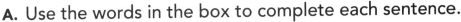

> carbon dioxide   dissolved   air pressure

1. Soda is a mixture of gas _____ in liquid.

2. The _____ bubbles inside a can of soda try to escape.

3. The pressure inside a full can of soda is greater than the _____ outside.

B. Write **true** or **false**.

1. Air pressure always stays the same.   _____

2. A full balloon has more pressure inside it than outside of it.   _____

3. When a tire goes flat, the air pressure inside it becomes the same as the air pressure outside.   _____

C. Is there more air pressure on top of a mountain or at the beach? Explain your answer.

_____

_____

Air is a gas that surrounds us, takes up space, and creates weather.

Week 3

Where does wind come from?

This week, students will learn that wind results from air that is heated and cooled. Rays from the sun heat air. This causes the air molecules to spread farther apart, which lowers the air pressure and causes the warm air to rise. As the warm air rises, cooler, denser air moves in to take its place. This moving air is what we feel as wind. Scientists have found that large patterns of wind are fairly constant around the globe. They study these winds, called prevailing winds, to see where massive weather events such as large thunderstorms will likely travel.

Day One

Vocabulary:
meteorologist, pressure system

Distribute page 111 and introduce the vocabulary. Then have volunteers read the introduction aloud. If necessary, review the meanings of *clockwise* and *counterclockwise*. Then guide students through the map on the page, explaining that maps like these help meteorologists predict the weather. Explain that "H" means a high pressure system and "L" means a low pressure system. Then have students complete the activity.

Day Two

Vocabulary: *circulate*

Distribute page 112 and introduce the vocabulary word. Then have volunteers read the introduction aloud. Guide students through the diagram and point out the warm air rising and the cold air moving in to take its place. Have students complete the activity. Then review answers together. For the oral activity, pair students or discuss the question as a group. Remind students that wind needs both warm and cool air to form.

Day Three

Vocabulary:
anemometer, wind vane

Ask: **If we can't see wind, how do we measure it?** Distribute page 113 and introduce the vocabulary. Then have volunteers read the introduction aloud. Point out the pictures of the anemometer and wind vane and invite students to hypothesize how they work. (The wind vane is blown by the wind and points in the direction the wind is blowing, while the anemometer spins at different speeds depending on the strength of the wind.) Then have students complete the activity.

Day Four

Distribute page 114 and have volunteers read the introduction aloud. Invite students to name other things that the wind does or helps us do. (e.g., fly a kite, play wind chimes, etc.) Have students complete the activity. For the oral activity, pair students or discuss the question as a group.

Day Five

Tell students they will review what they have learned about wind. Have them complete page 115. Go over the answers together.

Name _____

Day 1

Weekly Question

Where does wind come from?

Wind is the movement of air. Wind blows during storms and on clear, sunny days. It can be hot or cold. It blows at different speeds, too. People who study wind and weather are called **meteorologists**. They study how wind moves around the planet.

Meteorologists also study **pressure systems**. In high pressure systems, there is more air pressure than normal, and the wind blows clockwise. High pressure systems usually have good weather. In low pressure systems, there is less air pressure than normal, and the wind blows counterclockwise. Low pressure systems usually cause storms.

Draw arrows to show the direction that the wind is blowing in each pressure system. Then answer the questions below.

Vocabulary

meteorologist
a person who studies wind and weather

pressure system
regions of air with more high or low air pressure than normal

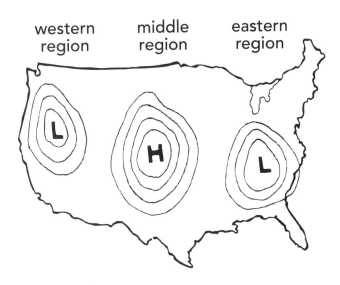

western region   middle region   eastern region

1. How many pressure systems does the map show? _____

2. Which region probably has good weather? _____

3. Which way do you think wind in a hurricane blows, **clockwise** or **counterclockwise**? _____

Name _____

Weekly Question

Day 2

Where does wind come from?

You know that the sun is an important source of energy on Earth. During the daytime, energy from the sun heats the land and the water. The land and water then heat the air above them. Warm air weighs less than cold air, so the warm air rises. Less air means that there is less air pressure. Colder air moves in to take the place of the warm air that rose and left. The air begins to **circulate**, and this causes wind.

Vocabulary

circulate
to move in a circle

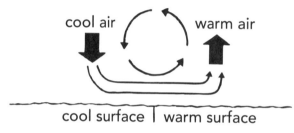

cool air   warm air

cool surface | warm surface

Write complete sentences to answer the questions.

1. How does the sun help create wind? _____

_____

2. Why will warm air rise above cooler air? _____

_____

3. If there is less air in a certain place, is there more or less pressure?

_____

Talk

"The Doldrums" is a very warm area in the ocean near the equator. Sometimes there is no wind for weeks at a time. Why do you think this is? Discuss it with a partner.

Name _____

Day 3

Weekly Question

Where does wind come from?

When the wind changes speed and direction, it often brings a change in the weather. This is why meteorologists use special tools to measure wind speed and direction.

A **wind vane** is a device that points in the direction the wind is blowing from. Another device, called an **anemometer** (ann-ih-MOM-uh-tur), is used to measure how fast the wind is blowing. The faster the anemometer spins, the faster the wind is blowing. Without these tools, it would be difficult to measure wind. It would be difficult to measure how strong a storm is or to know the direction it is moving in.

Vocabulary

anemometer
a tool that measures wind speed

wind vane
a tool that shows the direction that the wind is blowing

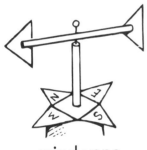

wind vane

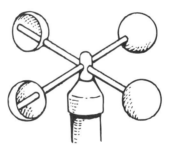

anemometer

Help each student figure out which tool he or she needs to study the wind. Write **anemometer** or **wind vane**.

1. Maria wants to know which direction
   the wind is blowing.   _____

2. Craig needs to measure how fast the wind
   is blowing.   _____

3. Kim needs to check if the wind is blowing
   faster or slower than 8 miles per hour.   _____

4. Rachel wants to know if the wind is
   traveling east or west.   _____

Name _____

Day 4

Weekly Question

Where does wind come from?

Wind is an important resource. We use it to create power. Sails catch wind to help boats move. People use wind to dry their clothes outside. Windmills are used to pump water from the ground. Today we even have wind farms. Wind moves giant machines, called turbines (TUR-byns), that turn to make electricity. The largest wind farm is in Texas. It has over 400 turbines. That is enough to make electricity for 20,000 homes!

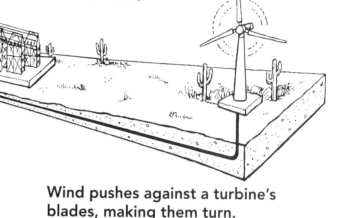

Wind pushes against a turbine's blades, making them turn.

Write **true** or **false**.

1. Wind moves a boat by pushing against its sails. _____

2. A windmill uses wind to create water. _____

3. We can use the wind to power homes. _____

4. A turbine's blades need wind to turn them. _____

Talk

Some people like wind power because it is clean and we will never run out of it. Other people don't like wind power because birds can can get caught in the blades and the turbines are expensive to build. How do you feel about wind power? Discuss it with a partner.

Name _____

Day 5

Weekly Question

Where does wind come from?

A. Use the words in the box to complete the sentences.

> anemometers   circulates
> meteorologists   wind vanes
> pressure systems

1. _____ study weather and the wind.

2. When air _____, it begins to move around.

3. We use _____ to measure wind speed.

4. _____ show the direction of the wind.

5. Low _____ often bring storms.

B. Use the words in the box to label the diagram.

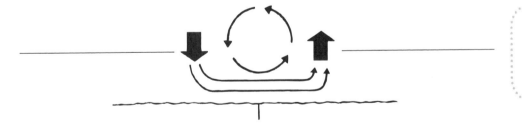

> warm air
>
> cool air

C. Write **true** or **false**.

1. Cold air always rises. _____

2. Wind can help us create electricity. _____

3. Warm air weighs less than cold air. _____

Big Idea 4

Air is a gas that surrounds us, takes up space, and creates weather.

Week 4

How do birds fly?

While mechanical flight is a relatively recent development for people, birds have been flying for millions of years. This week, students will learn that birds' bodies have many adaptations that make this possible, including light bones, strong breast muscles, and feathers that help trap air to make lift and gliding easier. The three principle forces at work in flight are lift, drag, and thrust. Lift carries birds up and keeps them aloft. Drag is the friction of the air as it pulls on birds' bodies, much in the same way water slows down a swimmer. Thrust is the force of moving forward, which birds create when they flap their wings. Birds' bodies are shaped to minimize drag, and their muscles are developed to maximize thrust.

Day One

Vocabulary: *adaptations*

Invite students to explain how they think birds fly. Then distribute page 117 and introduce the vocabulary word. Have volunteers read the introduction aloud. Explain that while wings are very important, almost every part of a bird's body has adapted to help it fly. Have students complete the activities. Review the answers together.

Day Two

Vocabulary: *drag, lift, thrust*

Distribute page 118 and have volunteers read the introduction aloud. As the concepts of *thrust*, *drag*, and *lift* are described, call students' attention to the labels on the diagram that show these forces. Then have students complete the activity. Review the answers together.

Day Three

Vocabulary: *thermal current*

Materials: pictures of gliders (optional)

Distribute page 119 and introduce the vocabulary word. Have volunteers read the introduction aloud. Remind students that sunlight heats the air and causes it to rise. This creates wind and thermals, which many birds use to glide. Have students complete activity A independently. For activity B, you may wish to show students pictures of gliders to help them answer the question.

Day Four

Materials: pictures of birds with various wing sizes

Distribute page 120 and have volunteers read the introduction aloud. If you have pictures of birds with different wing sizes, display them and discuss with students how each bird flies. Then have students complete the chart. Review the answers together.

Day Five

Tell students they will review what they have learned about air and flight. Then have them complete page 121. Go over the answers together.

Name _____

Day 1

Weekly Question

How do birds fly?

People have always been interested in how birds fly. For centuries, people have tried to build wings and soar through the air. But there's a lot more to flying than just having a pair of wings.

Birds have many special **adaptations** to help them fly. Birds have very strong muscles that help them flap their wings. And birds' bones are hollow, so they weigh less. Birds also have feathers that catch and use air to make flying easier. In fact, air pressure plays a key role in making flight possible for birds.

Vocabulary

adaptations
changes to an animal's body that help it survive

A. Complete the labels on the diagram to describe three adaptations that help birds fly.

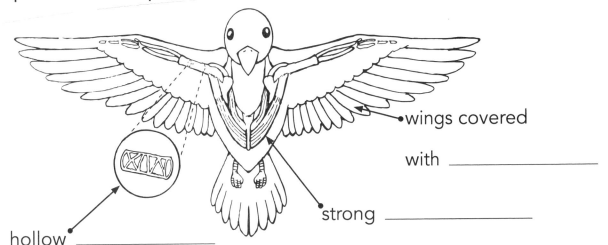

wings covered

with _____

strong _____

hollow _____

B. Write **true** or **false**.

1. Adaptations help all animals fly.   _____

2. Birds' bones weigh less than people's bones.   _____

3. Wings are the only thing needed for flight.   _____

Name _____

Day 2

Weekly Question

How do birds fly?

When a bird flaps its wings, it uses power to move it forward. This is called **thrust**. But as the bird flies, the air around it slows the bird down. This is called **drag**. Drag slows down anything that flies through the air.

To overcome drag, a bird's wing is curved. Air flows over and under it. Air moving above and over the wing has lower pressure. The air below the wing has higher pressure. This creates a force known as **lift**.

Vocabulary

drag
the force of air pushing against a flying animal or object

lift
air pressure under a flying animal or object that lifts it higher

thrust
forward movement by a flying animal or object

Use the diagram to help you answer the questions below.

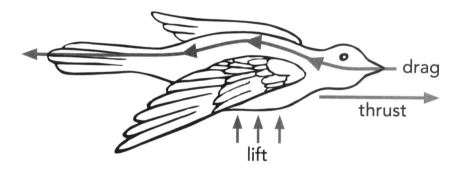

1. Where is air pressure the lowest, over or under a bird's wing?

   _____

2. Where is air pressure the greatest, under or over a bird's wing?

   _____

3. What is the forward movement of a bird called?

   _____

4. If air causes drag on a bird, what causes drag on a fish?

   _____

Name _____

Day 3

Weekly Question

How do birds fly?

When birds are flying, they can't spend the whole time flapping their wings. They would become too tired! One way they can rest is to ride on **thermal currents**. These are rising columns of warm air. Remember that warm air weighs less than cool air, so it rises. This gives birds an extra lift without any extra flapping. If you have ever seen a hawk circling in the sky, you were watching it ride a thermal current.

Vocabulary

thermal current
a column of warm, rising air

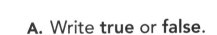

A. Write **true** or **false**.

1. A thermal current is a current of warm air. _____

2. Birds flap more when they ride thermal currents. _____

3. A hawk will gain lift when it is riding
   on a thermal current. _____

4. Using thermal currents is a good way for hawks
   to save energy. _____

B. Gliders are like airplanes but with no engines. They can fly, but they can remain in the air only for a short time. How do you think they stay in the air? Explain your answer.

_____

Name _____

Day 4

Weekly Question

How do birds fly?

The size of wings can affect how a bird flies. Long wings are good for soaring long distances. Eagles spend a lot of time in the air looking for food, so they have long wings. Sparrows, which eagles sometimes hunt, have short wings. Short wings allow a bird to fly short distances quickly, and with bursts of speed. This is helpful for birds that want to avoid larger animals.

Read the description of each bird. Then write the type of wings it needs: long or short.

Bird	What It Does	Type of Wings
Canada Goose	migrates a great distance from Canada to southern United States	
Sparrow	darts from perch to perch and does not migrate	
Albatross	travels long distances, gliding on ocean winds	
Wren	flits from bush to bush, trying to catch insects	

Name _____

Day 5 *Weekly Question*

How do birds fly?

A. Use the words in the box to complete each sentence.

> adaptation   drag   thermal   lift   thrust

1. A _____ current allows birds to fly higher and with less work.

2. Differences in air pressure above and below a bird's wings create _____.

3. The force that slows down a bird is called _____.

4. A bird uses its strong muscles to create _____.

5. Feathers are one _____ that helps a bird fly.

B. Circle the correct answer.

1. A bird only needs feathers to fly.   true   false

2. Flapping wings takes less energy than soaring.   true   false

3. Warm air is useful to migrating birds.   true   false

C. Label the arrows to show where **drag**, **thrust**, and **lift** are happening.

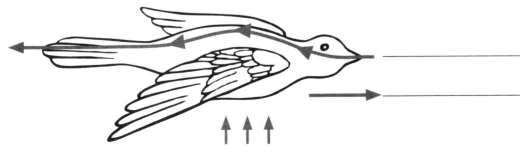

_____

Name _____

Unit Review

Comprehension

All About Air

Read each item. Fill in the bubble next to the correct answer.

1. Which of these is true about warm air?

   Ⓐ It falls to the ground.

   Ⓑ It rises in the atmosphere.

   Ⓒ It stays at sea level.

   Ⓓ It weighs more than cold air.

2. Which of these altitudes has the most amount of oxygen?

   Ⓐ sea level

   Ⓑ 10,000 feet above sea level

   Ⓒ 6,000 feet above sea level

   Ⓓ outer space

3. Which of these is an example of low pressure?

   Ⓐ a pressure system with good weather

   Ⓑ a hurricane

   Ⓒ an unopened can of soda

   Ⓓ a tire filled with air

4. Air under a bird's wing gives it _____.

   Ⓐ thermals

   Ⓑ thrust

   Ⓒ drag

   Ⓓ lift

5. Warm and cool air circulate to form _____.

   Ⓐ pressure

   Ⓑ altitude

   Ⓒ molecules

   Ⓓ wind

Daily Science • EMC 5013 • © Evan-Moor Corp.

Name _____

Unit Review

Vocabulary

Either/Or Questions

Daily Science

Big Idea 4

WEEK 5

Write the underlined words that answer the questions below.

1. What does **altitude** describe, <u>how high</u>
   a plane is or <u>how fast</u> it is going?   _____

2. Does a **thermal current** help birds <u>fly</u> or <u>stay warm</u>?   _____

3. If something is **dissolved**, is it <u>floating on</u> a
   liquid or <u>mixed into</u> a liquid?   _____

4. Does a **meteorologist** study <u>weather</u> or <u>rocks</u>?   _____

5. Which one measures **wind speed**, a <u>wind vane</u>
   or an <u>anemometer</u>?   _____

6. What moves a bird **forward**, <u>thrust</u> or <u>drag</u>?   _____

7. Does **circulation** describe moving in
   a <u>straight line</u> or in a <u>circle</u>?   _____

8. If you were at **sea level**, would you be in
   the <u>mountains</u> or in a <u>valley</u>?   _____

9. Does **lift** help a plane <u>fly</u> or <u>land</u>?   _____

10. Is the **atmosphere** in <u>outer space</u> or
    <u>close to Earth</u>?   _____

11. Is the **air pressure** in a flat tire <u>high</u> or <u>low</u>?   _____

12. Are **carbon dioxide** and **oxygen** <u>liquids</u> or <u>gases</u>?   _____

13. Which one is an example of an **adaptation**,
    a bird's <u>feathers</u> or a bird's <u>habitat</u>?   _____

14. Does a **pressure system** affect the <u>air</u>
    or the <u>ground</u>?   _____

Name _____

The people who invented airplanes studied how birds fly. Even today, airplanes are still built like giant metal birds. They have wings and a tail, and they use the forces of air to fly the same way that birds do.

Look at the pictures of the airplanes below. On the first airplane, label each **wing** and the **tail**. On the second airplane, label each arrow to tell whether it is showing **thrust**, **drag**, or **lift**.

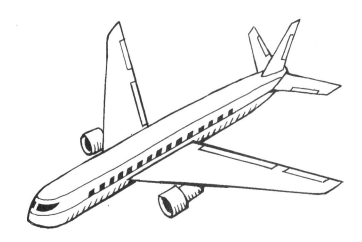

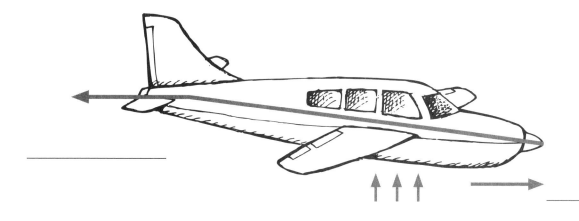

Name _____

Hands-on Activity
Tornado in a Bottle

Tornadoes are strong, rotating winds that form when a storm causes air to rise very quickly. You can create a "mini-tornado" by using two plastic bottles. Look carefully to see the rotating motion that a tornado makes.

What You Need

- two clear plastic bottles, empty
- waterproof tape
- water

1. Make sure the bottles are clean, and peel off any labels.

2. Fill one of the bottles two-thirds full with water.

3. Cover the mouth of the empty bottle with tape and poke a hole in it. Holes of different sizes will create "tornadoes" with different features.

4. Use tape to fasten the bottles together at the mouth, with the empty one on top. Use enough tape so that no water will leak out.

5. Turn the bottles over so that the water is on the top.

6. Immediately swirl the bottles.

What Did You Discover?

1. What happens to the water as it flows from the top bottle into the bottom bottle?

   _____

2. A tornado happens in air, and a whirlpool happens in water. How do you think they are alike?

   _____

Big Idea 5

Light travels in a straight line until it hits an object. Light can be absorbed, refracted, or reflected.

Key Concept

Light

National Standard

Light travels in a straight line until it hits an object. Light can be reflected, refracted, or absorbed.

By third grade, students should have a basic understanding that sunlight is energy we can see and feel. But students may not understand the properties of light: absorption, reflection, and refraction. This Big Idea teaches students that:

→ light travels in a ray that passes through translucent objects and is absorbed by opaque objects;

→ light can be absorbed, refracted, and reflected;

→ light travels in a straight line; and

→ lenses bend light and magnify or project images.

Teacher Background

It is easy to observe light, but it is often difficult to understand light's properties. This unit focuses on how light travels as a ray. This means that light travels in a straight line and can be absorbed, refracted, and reflected.

When light is absorbed, it is usually converted into another form of energy, such as heat. It can also become electrical energy, such as when solar panels convert sunlight into electricity.

When light hits an object, the object changes the light's path. This is called refraction or reflection. Objects with flat, polished surfaces reflect light, sending it back the way it came. But other things, such as water, can refract light. This is what makes a straw look bent in a glass of water. Light can also be refracted by lenses, which will cause images to appear distorted. This is helpful when we want to enlarge images or project them onto a screen.

For specific background information on each week's concepts, refer to the notes on pp. 128, 134, 140, and 146.

Unit Overview

WEEK 1: Why does it get hot in a car on a sunny day when it is cold outside?

Connection to the Big Idea: Light is a form of energy that can be absorbed.

Students learn that light travels in a straight line until it hits another object. They discover that light passes through transparent objects, but it is absorbed by opaque objects. They then understand how parts of a car absorb energy and become hot, and that this is the same thing that occurs in greenhouses.

Content Vocabulary: *absorb, opaque, radiate, ray, translucent, transparent*

WEEK 2: Why does a straw look bent in a glass of water?

Connection to the Big Idea: Refracted light causes image distortion.

Students learn that light causes a straw to look bent in a glass. Students then learn that lenses will refract light, too, and can be useful in tools such as telescopes and microscopes.

Content Vocabulary: *distort, focus, lens, refract*

WEEK 3: How does a movie projector work?

Connection to the Big Idea: A movie projector relies on several properties of light to work.

Students learn that projectors are machines that use lenses and light to project film images onto a screen. They learn that the light shines brightly through the projector, and the lens helps focus the image. Finally, they discover that the moving images we see are a series of still pictures run very quickly through the machine.

Content Vocabulary: *film, projector*

WEEK 4: How do mirrors work?

Connection to the Big Idea: Mirrors reflect light rays.

Students learn that light rays can reflect and travel in a new direction. They then study how mirrors work to reflect light and create reflections. Students expand their understanding by learning that light will reflect off many flat, polished objects. Finally, students discover that mirrors, if bent like lenses, will distort reflections.

Content Vocabulary: *polish, reflect, reflection*

WEEK 5: Unit Review

You may choose to do these activities to review concepts of light.

p. 152: Comprehension Students answer multiple-choice questions about key concepts from the unit.

p. 153: Vocabulary Students complete a crossword puzzle using key vocabulary from the unit.

p. 154: Visual Literacy Students study a picture and answer questions about how light is behaving.

p. 155: Hands-on Activity Students use water to magnify images. Instructions and materials are listed on the student page.

Big Idea 5

Light travels in a straight line until it hits an object. Light can be absorbed, refracted, or reflected.

Week 1

Why does it get hot in a car on a sunny day when it is cold outside?

In this week's lesson, students learn that sunlight is a form of energy. Like all forms of energy, light can be transformed into other forms of energy, such as heat. So a car sitting out in the sun will get hot because sunlight is converted to heat. The windows of the car allow the sunlight to come into the car. The car's dashboard and upholstery absorb the sunlight, and when this happens, the energy from the sunlight is converted to heat. If the car's windows are closed, the heat has no way to escape, so the car becomes hot. Students will also learn that this is basically the way a greenhouse works. You may wish to expand on the concept by discussing the term *greenhouse effect*, which students may have heard in reference to climate change.

Day One Vocabulary: *radiate, ray*	Distribute page 129 and introduce the vocabulary. Have volunteers read the introduction aloud. You may want to use the picture to review how, as Earth orbits the sun, different parts of Earth get more or less sunlight. Then have students complete the activities. Review the answers together.
Day Two Vocabulary: *absorb, opaque, transparent*	Distribute page 130 and introduce the vocabulary. Point out different objects in the classroom and have students say whether they are transparent or opaque. Then have volunteers read the introduction aloud. Invite students to describe the experience of getting into a hot car and to explain what they usually do to cool off the car. (e.g., roll down the windows) Then have students complete the activities.
Day Three Vocabulary: *translucent*	Distribute page 131 and introduce the vocabulary word. Have volunteers read the introduction aloud. Then invite students to point out any objects in the classroom that are translucent, or to think of other translucent things. (e.g., waxed paper, stained glass, thin curtains) Then have students complete the activities. Review the answers together.
Day Four	Distribute page 132 and have volunteers read the introduction aloud. Invite students who have been in a greenhouse to describe what it was like inside. Then have students complete the activities. Review the answers together.
Day Five	Tell students that they will review everything they have learned about sunlight and how light travels. Then have them complete page 133. Go over the answers together.

Name _____

Day 1

Weekly Question

Why does it get hot in a car on a sunny day when it is cold outside?

When we think of sunshine, we think of bright, warm days. The sun supplies Earth with a lot of energy. We see that energy as light and feel it as heat. Sunlight **radiates** out from the sun in all directions in the form of **rays**. These rays, like all forms of light, travel in straight lines.

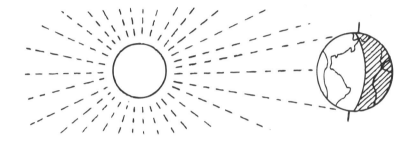

Vocabulary

radiate
to spread out in all directions

ray
a thin beam of light

A. Write **true** or **false**.

1. Sunlight travels in straight lines. _____

2. Light and heat are two forms of energy. _____

3. Light radiates from only one side of the sun. _____

B. Use the words in the box to complete the paragraph.

> **radiate   ray   energy   sunlight**

Light and heat are forms of _____ that

_____ from the sun. Every _____

of _____ that hits Earth helps keep our

planet alive.

Name _____

Day 2

Weekly Question

Why does it get hot in a car on a sunny day when it is cold outside?

When a ray of sunlight hits a **transparent** object, such as a window, it passes through the object. If a ray hits an **opaque** object, such as a wall, the object **absorbs** the sun's energy. A car's windows are transparent, but the things inside, such as the seats and dashboard, are opaque. They absorb the sun's energy. Heat builds up in the car.

A. Look at each object below. Write whether it is **transparent** or **opaque**.

1.  _____

2. _____

3.  _____

4.  _____

Vocabulary

absorb
to soak up or take in completely

opaque
something that does not allow light to pass through it

transparent
something that allows light to pass through it

B. Number the steps below in the correct order to show how a car gets hot inside.

____ The temperature inside the car goes up.

____ Things inside the car absorb the light and heat.

____ Sunlight shines on the car.

____ The light passes through the windshield.

Name _____

Day 3

Weekly Question

Why does it get hot in a car on a sunny day when it is cold outside?

If an object lets through some but not all light, is the object transparent or opaque? Actually, it's **translucent**. Tinted windows, sunglasses, and lampshades are some examples of translucent objects. We use translucent objects to partially block or scatter light that is too bright.

Vocabulary

translucent
something that allows only some light to pass through it

A. Circle the picture in each pair that shows something translucent.

 1.

2.

3.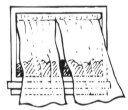

B. Answer the questions.

1. On a hot day, would you rather be riding in a bus with **tinted** windows or **clear** windows? Explain.

_____

2. Would you rather have sunglasses with **translucent** lenses or **opaque** lenses? Explain.

_____

Name _____

Weekly Question

Why does it get hot in a car on a sunny day when it is cold outside?

Not only can the sun heat the inside of a car on a cold day, but it can help plants grow in cold weather. Many people use a greenhouse in the winter to grow plants. A greenhouse has transparent glass or plastic walls that let in a lot of sunlight. The objects inside absorb the sun's energy and build up heat, even if the air outside is cold. Plants that need a lot of light and warmth to grow, such as tomatoes and most flowers, are often grown in greenhouses.

A. Read each cause. Check the box next to the correct effect.

1. **Cause:** Sunlight shines on a greenhouse.

   Effect: ☐ The walls of the greenhouse block the light.
   ☐ The light passes through the walls of the greenhouse.

2. **Cause:** Opaque objects in a greenhouse absorb sunlight.

   Effect: ☐ The air in the greenhouse warms up.
   ☐ The air in the greenhouse cools down.

3. **Cause:** The greenhouse is warm and brightly lit.

   Effect: ☐ Tomatoes growing in the greenhouse get ripe.
   ☐ Tomatoes growing in the greenhouse die.

B. Some greenhouses have translucent instead of transparent walls. Why do you think this is? When might translucent walls be better?

_____

_____

Name _____

Day 5

Weekly Question
Why does it get hot in a car on a sunny day when it is cold outside?

A. Write whether each object is **opaque**, **translucent**, or **transparent**.

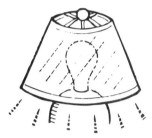 

_____   _____   _____

B. Use the words in the box to complete the sentences.

> **absorb**   **opaque**   **ray**   **translucent**   **transparent**

1. Light passes completely through _____ objects.

2. Light does not pass through _____ objects.

3. A car's dashboard will _____ light.

4. Some light will pass through _____ objects.

5. Light travels in a straight line called a _____.

C. Check the box next to the car that will be hotter on a sunny day.

☐ 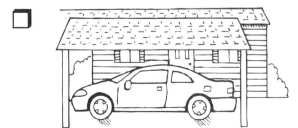   ☐

Daily Science

Big Idea 5

Light travels in a straight line until it hits an object. Light can be absorbed, refracted, or reflected.

Week 2

Why does a straw look bent in a glass of water?

This week, students learn what happens when light passes through different materials. When a light ray travels through transparent materials, its path can change direction, or be "bent." This is called refraction. Some materials, such as glass, don't cause a large amount of refraction unless they are curved, as in the case of a lens. Other materials, such as water, can refract light a great deal. This is why a straw looks bent in a glass of water and why lenses can magnify or focus an image.

Day One Vocabulary: *refract*	Distribute page 135, introduce the vocabulary word, and have volunteers read the introduction aloud. Use the diagram in activity A to reinforce the concept of how light rays get refracted when they pass through water. Then have students complete the activities. Review the answers together.
Day Two Materials: straw; glass of water; blue, green, and yellow crayons	Distribute page 136 and have volunteers read the introduction aloud. Then display a glass of water with a straw in it. Give students a chance to study it and then describe what they see. Use the diagram in activity A to explain that light rays are traveling from behind the glass. The rays going through the water get refracted before they reach the eye. Then distribute crayons and have students complete the activities independently.
Day Three Vocabulary: *lens, focus*	Distribute page 137, introduce the vocabulary, and have volunteers read the introduction aloud. You might ask students with glasses to allow the class to compare the thicknesses of the lenses and draw conclusions about why they might be different. Then have students complete the activities.
Day Four Vocabulary: *distort*	Distribute page 138 and introduce the vocabulary word. Then have volunteers read the introduction aloud. Invite students who have looked through a microscope or a telescope to describe what they saw. Then brainstorm other tools that help us see. (e.g., magnifying glass, binoculars, periscope) Have students complete the activities. Review the answers together, emphasizing in activity B that looking at the sun is dangerous.
Day Five	Tell students they will review everything they have learned about refraction. Have them complete page 139. Go over the answers together.

Name _____

Weekly Question

Day 1

Why does a straw look bent in a glass of water?

Our eyes work by gathering light. If you can see an object, that means light rays are traveling from that object toward your eyes. But sometimes light passes through something else that **refracts** the rays, or bends them, before they reach your eyes. For example, light can't pass from air through water in a straight line. When light hits water, it gets refracted.

Vocabulary

refract
to bend

A. The diagram below shows how light refracts. Study it and then answer the questions.

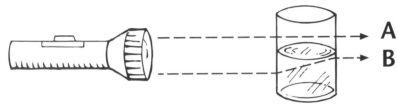

1. Which ray is being refracted, **A** or **B**? _____

2. Which ray does not change its path? Why? _____

_____

B. Fill in the bubble next to each correct answer.

1. The word **refract** means to _____.

  Ⓐ pass through   Ⓒ block

  Ⓑ bend   Ⓓ bounce back

2. Our eyes help us see by _____ light.

  Ⓐ producing   Ⓒ gathering

  Ⓑ separating   Ⓓ shutting out

Name _____

Have you ever noticed that when you look through a window on a rainy day, it's hard to see clearly through the raindrops on the glass? That's because even though water is transparent, it refracts light and blurs what you see. A similar thing happens when you look at a straw in a glass of water. Light rays traveling through the water refract and trick your eye into thinking the straw looks bent.

A. Look at the diagram. Color the straw above the water blue. Color the straw below the water green. Use yellow to trace the ray of light that is refracted.

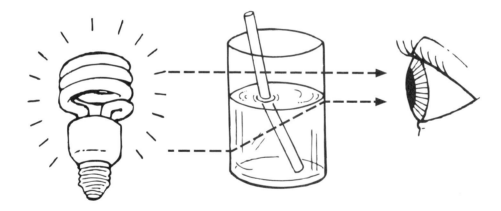

B. Look at the diagram again. Write **true** or **false**.

1. The water is bending the straw.   _____

2. The eye can see only the part of the straw that is above water.   _____

3. If the glass was empty, the straw would not look bent.   _____

Name _____

Day 3

Weekly Question

Why does a straw look bent in a glass of water?

Water isn't the only thing that will refract light. Glass will, too. Glass that is thick or curved will cause light to bend more than a thin, flat sheet of glass will. That's how eyeglasses work. The curve of the **lenses** refracts the light that passes through them and helps **focus** the rays onto the correct spot on the eyes so they can see a clear picture.

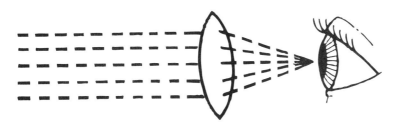

A. Complete the paragraph. Use words from the passage.

Eyeglasses work by refracting light through

curved _____. This focuses the

light as it reaches the person's _____.

Vocabulary

lens
a curved piece of clear glass or plastic that makes an object look bigger or more in focus

focus
to make an image clearer by making spread-out light rays come together at a point

B. Fill in the bubble next to the correct answer.

1. Which of these would refract light the LEAST?

Ⓐ a glass of water   Ⓑ a window   Ⓒ a block of ice

2. Why do you think some people's eyeglasses have thicker lenses than others?

Ⓐ Thicker lenses look better on those people.

Ⓑ Some people have bigger eyes than others.

Ⓒ Some people have worse eyesight than others.

Name _____

Weekly Question
Why does a straw look bent in a glass of water?

Sometimes refracted light **distorts**, or gets in the way of, what we are trying to see. But other times refraction comes in handy! It makes eyeglasses possible, and it gives us tools such as microscopes and telescopes. The lenses in microscopes make tiny objects appear large enough for our eyes to see. The lenses in telescopes give us a closer look at objects that are far away.

Vocabulary

distort
to change how something appears, making it look unclear or different

microscope

telescope

A. Name four tools that use lenses to help us see things better.

1. _____   3. _____

2. _____   4. _____

B. Accidentally glancing at the sun can bother your eyes for a few minutes. But looking at the sun through a telescope will cause permanent damage. Why do you think that is?

_____

_____

Name _____

Day 5

Weekly Question
Why does a straw look bent in a glass of water?

A. Circle the word that completes each sentence.

1. If a ray of light is refracted, it is _____.

straight   bent

2. Glass will refract the most light if it is _____.

curved   flat

3. A telescope makes objects look _____.

closer   smaller

B. Draw light rays in the picture below to show how eyeglasses work.

C. Use the words in the box to complete the sentences.

focus

distorts

lens

1. A microscope has a special _____ that makes objects look larger.

2. When you look at an object through a glass of water, the water _____ how the object looks.

3. A lens helps _____ light rays on your eye.

Daily Science

Big Idea 5

Light travels in a straight line until it hits an object. Light can be absorbed, refracted, or reflected.

Week 3

How does a movie projector work?

Students may be unfamiliar with the concept of a film projector, having seen only DVD players, VCRs, or streaming video. However, most movies in theaters are still shown with a film projector, which utilizes several key properties of light in order to project an image onto a screen and thereby helps to demonstrate the concepts that students have been learning. Light travels from a light bulb in a straight line through translucent film, and then through the lens of a projector. The projector refracts the light and increases the size of the image to fill the screen.

Day One

Vocabulary: *film, projector*

Distribute page 141 and introduce the vocabulary. Activate prior knowledge by having students discuss any film, slide, or overhead projectors they have seen. Then have volunteers read the introduction aloud. Use the diagram in activity A to discuss the parts of a projector. Then have students complete the activities. Review the answers together.

Day Two

Distribute page 142. Have volunteers read the introduction aloud. Remind students that light and heat are both forms of energy. Then have students complete the activities. Review the answers together.

Day Three

Materials: overhead projector (optional)

Distribute page 143 and have volunteers read the introduction aloud. If you have an overhead projector, you may wish to use it to demonstrate how to focus an image. Then guide students through the diagrams in activity A, helping them understand how light rays need to spread out instead of come together in order to make an image larger. Have students complete the other activities independently. Review the answers together.

Day Four

Materials: flipbook made from a sticky notepad

Ahead of time, make a simple flipbook from a sticky notepad. On each page, draw a stick figure that looks like it is walking, with each picture showing a small change in body position. Then distribute page 144 and have volunteers read the introduction aloud. Show students the flipbook and allow them to take turns flipping through it and observing what they see. Then have students complete the activities. For activity A, you may first want to review the terms *transparent*, *translucent*, and *opaque*.

Day Five

Tell students they will review everything they have learned about movie projectors. Have them complete page 145. Review the answers together.

Name _____

Day 1

Weekly Question

How does a movie projector work?

If you have ever been to a movie theater, you saw a movie projected onto a huge screen by a special machine called a **projector**. This machine shines light through **film** that is passing through the machine quickly. The machine uses a lens to change the tiny pictures on the film into giant images that fill the screen.

A. The diagram below shows a very simple projector. Label the **lens**, **film**, and **light bulb**.

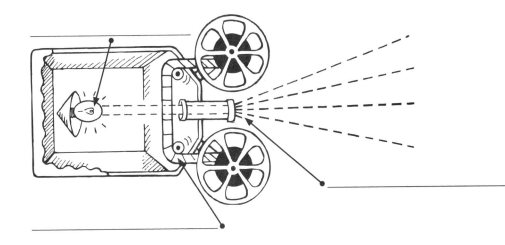

Vocabulary

film
a thin strip of coated material with images on it

projector
a machine that passes light through film and a lens to project images onto a screen

B. Write **true** or **false**.

1. Movie projectors make big images smaller. _____

2. A movie projector has a lens and a light bulb. _____

3. Light shines through the film before reaching the lens. _____

4. The lens of a projector has tiny pictures on it. _____

Name _____

Day 2

Weekly Question

How does a movie projector work?

The light bulb inside a projector is very bright. In fact, it shines brighter than most bulbs found in your house. Because the light is so bright, the bulb gets very hot. However, the light from a projector gets less bright as it travels to the screen. With other lights on, the image is hard to see. That's why movies are shown in the dark.

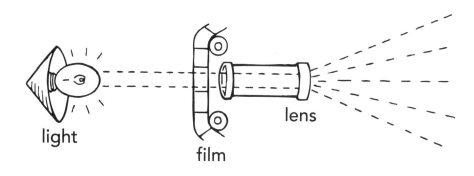

light

film

lens

A. What types of energy does the light bulb in a movie projector produce?

1. _____   **2.** _____

B. Answer each question.

1. Why do you suppose movie theaters don't have windows?

_____

_____

2. If the film stopped moving in a projector, it would melt. Why do you think this happens?

_____

Name _____

Day 3

Weekly Question

How does a movie projector work?

As film moves through a projector, light passes from the bulb through the film and then through a lens. The lens refracts the light, making the image on the film much, much bigger. The lens can also be adjusted, or moved. This changes how the light is refracted and focuses the image so that it looks clearer to us on the screen.

A. Circle the diagram that correctly shows how a projector lens refracts light.

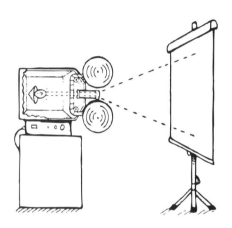
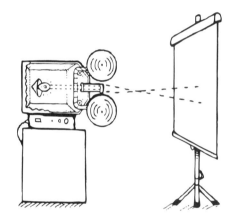

B. Name something with a lens that you have to focus in order to use.

_____

C. Many classrooms have an overhead projector, which passes light through a transparency and shows it on a screen or wall. Explain how you think an overhead projector is like a movie projector.

_____

_____

Weekly Question

Day 4

How does a movie projector work?

Daily Science

Big Idea 5

WEEK 3

Movie film is a long, translucent strip of tiny pictures, each called a frame. As film moves through a projector, the frames pass in front of the light one at a time, flashing their picture briefly on the screen. But the film moves so fast that our eyes can't see the separate frames. The pictures blend together so that we think we are seeing moving objects.

A. Based on how a movie projector works, write whether each thing below is **transparent**, **translucent**, or **opaque**.

1. movie film _____

2. movie screen _____

3. projector lens _____

B. Number the frames to show the order in which they would appear on a strip of film.

_____   _____   _____   _____

Name _____

Day 5

Weekly Question

How does a movie projector work?

Daily Science

Big Idea 5

WEEK 3

A. Use the words in the box to complete the sentences.

focus   projector   film

1. A _____ is used to show a movie on a big screen.

2. As the _____ passes in front of the light, pictures are projected onto the screen.

3. If the picture on the screen looks unclear, you might need to _____ the lens.

B. Draw a line to show the path of light as it passes through the projector and onto the screen.

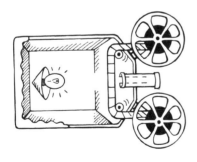

C. Scientists are working on new kinds of light bulbs that are bright but not hot. Do you think these bulbs use more or less energy than a movie projector bulb? Explain your answer.

_____

Light travels in a straight line until it hits an object. Light can be absorbed, refracted, or reflected.

Week 4
How do mirrors work?

This week, students will learn about reflection to further explore how light travels. Light reflects best when it strikes a polished, shiny surface such as a mirror, which is made of glass with a thin metal coating on one side of it. Light strikes and passes through the glass but is reflected by the metal. Anything that is smooth and polished has the potential to reflect light, including stone, wood, and bodies of water. Students will also learn how, just as curved glass *refracts* the light that passes through it and changes the image we see, a curved mirror *reflects* light in ways that change the reflection we see. A concave mirror will make the image smaller, while a convex mirror will expand the image.

Day One

Vocabulary: *reflect*

Materials: sheet of aluminum foil

Distribute page 147 and introduce the vocabulary word. Have volunteers read the introduction aloud. Review the definition of *opaque* if necessary, and then have students complete activity A. Discuss the answer together, asking volunteers to describe what is happening in each picture. (Light is traveling through transparent glass; light is being reflected; light is being absorbed by an opaque object.) Then have students complete activity B. Invite volunteers to read aloud their completed sentences. For activity C, show students a sheet of aluminum foil. Wad the foil into a ball and smooth it out again. Then have students write their responses.

Day Two

Vocabulary: *reflection*

Distribute page 148 and introduce the vocabulary word. Have students identify the base word in it. *(reflect)* Then have volunteers read the introduction aloud. Explain that we call glass "transparent" because it does a good job of letting light through, but that nothing is completely transparent—not even air. Have students complete the activities. For activity B, you might have students brainstorm in pairs or as a group before they write their responses.

Day Three

Vocabulary: *polish*

Distribute page 149 and introduce the vocabulary word. Then have volunteers read the introduction aloud. Have students complete the activities.

Day Four

Materials: large polished metal spoon

Distribute page 150 and have volunteers read the introduction aloud. Then have students complete the activities. For activity B, show students the spoon you brought in and allow them to examine its shape and reflective properties before answering the question.

Day Five

Tell students they will review everything they have learned about reflection. Have them complete page 151. Review the answers together.

Daily Science • EMC 5013 • © Evan-Moor Corp.

Name _____

Day 1

Weekly Question

How do mirrors work?

You know that opaque objects absorb light rather than letting the light pass through them. But what if an object is shiny, like a mirror or a piece of metal? Then the light ray will **reflect**, or bounce off the object, and travel in a new direction.

A. Check the box next to the picture that shows a light ray being reflected.

Vocabulary

reflect
to shine back

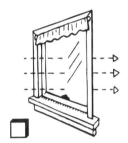 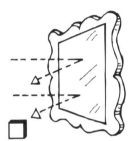 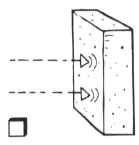

B. Use the words in the box to complete the sentences. You will need to use one word twice.

> absorbed   direction   reflected

1. Light is _____ by opaque objects,

   but it is _____ by mirrors.

2. When light is _____, the light ray will

   travel in a new _____.

C. Why do you think a crinkled sheet of aluminum foil does not reflect light as well as a smooth sheet? Explain.

_____

Name _____

A mirror is a piece of glass with metal on one side of it. The glass is transparent, but the metal is not. So when light passes through the glass and hits the metal, the light reflects back to you. Your eyes gather that light. You see your **reflection** in the mirror!

Vocabulary

reflection
the image you see in a mirror or other shiny surface

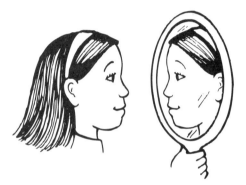

A. Write **true** or **false**.

1. The metal part of a mirror reflects light. _____

2. Glass absorbs all kinds of light. _____

3. You can see your reflection in a mirror when you stand behind the mirror. _____

4. A piece of glass with red paint on one side could be used as a mirror. _____

5. Your eyes can see light that is reflected. _____

B. Have you ever seen your reflection in something other than a mirror? Write two things besides mirrors that can show a reflection.

1. _____   2. _____

Name _____

Day 3

Weekly Question

How do mirrors work?

Daily Science

Big Idea 5

WEEK 4

Sometimes we see our reflection in windows or other glass objects, even though glass is transparent. How is this possible? Well, nothing is completely transparent. Most glass reflects some light back to you. Water, ice, metal, and even certain kinds of plastic also reflect light. What do these things have in common? They are all very smooth. You can make many things reflect light if you **polish** them.

Vocabulary

polish
to make something smooth and shiny by rubbing it

A. Which thing in each pair reflects more light? Check the box next to it.

1. ☐ a frozen pond
   ☐ a grassy field

3. ☐ an empty pool
   ☐ a pool full of swimmers

2. ☐ a brick wall
   ☐ a marble floor

4. ☐ a wooden spoon
   ☐ a silver spoon

B. Use the words in the box to complete the sentences. You will need to use one word twice.

> polish   transparent   reflection

1. If you _____ something enough, you can

   often see your _____ in it.

2. Nothing is completely _____. That is why

   you can sometimes see a _____ in a window.

Name _____

Day 4

Weekly Question

How do mirrors work?

   Have you ever looked at yourself in a fun-house mirror at a carnival? These mirrors are designed to stretch out your reflection in funny ways. They can make you look very tall and thin or very short and wide. How do they do this? They are curved like a lens. Just as a lens refracts the light that passes through it, a curved mirror reflects light rays in different directions, changing how you look.

A. Look at the curved mirrors below. Then answer each question.

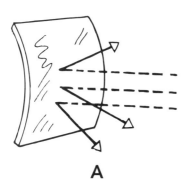

A

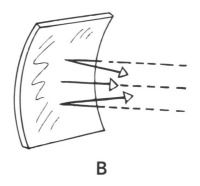

B

1. Would mirror **A** make you look smaller, bigger, or your actual size? _____

2. Would mirror **B** make you look smaller, bigger, or your actual size? _____

B. If you look at your reflection in a metal spoon, the image is distorted. Why do you think that is?

_____

Name _____

Day 5

Weekly Question
How do mirrors work?

A. Use the words in the box to complete the paragraph.

polish   reflect   reflection

The image you see in a mirror is a _____.

However, mirrors aren't the only things that _____

light. For example, if you _____ a stone until

it is very smooth, it will often reflect light.

B. Draw a picture of yourself standing in front of the mirror.
Then draw the reflection you see.

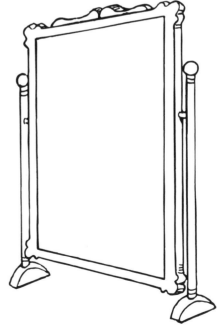

C. Name three things, other than a mirror, that reflect light.

1. _____   2. _____   3. _____

Name _____

Read each item. Fill in the bubble next to the correct answer.

1. Light would be completely absorbed by _____.

Ⓐ an opaque hat

Ⓑ a translucent curtain

Ⓒ a transparent jar

Ⓓ a polished mirror

2. Light rays that refract will _____.

Ⓐ stop moving

Ⓑ move along the same path

Ⓒ move along a different path

Ⓓ move backward

3. What does a movie projector need to work?

Ⓐ a light

Ⓑ some film

Ⓒ a lens

Ⓓ all of these

4. Which of these will NOT reflect light?

Ⓐ a small mirror

Ⓑ a rough stone

Ⓒ a shiny table

Ⓓ a clean window

5. Which part of a car is transparent?

Ⓐ the windshield

Ⓑ the door

Ⓒ the dashboard

Ⓓ the tires

6. Lenses _____ light rays.

Ⓐ absorb

Ⓑ block

Ⓒ create

Ⓓ refract

Name _____

Unit Review **Vocabulary** **Crossword Puzzle**

Daily Science

Big Idea 5

WEEK 5

Fill in the boxes with the correct vocabulary words.

absorb
focus
lens
opaque
projector
radiate
ray
reflect
refract
transparent

ACROSS

1. a device that shines images on a big screen

3. A light _____ travels in a straight line.

4. Some objects will completely soak up, or _____ light.

6. to travel in all directions

7. Something that doesn't allow light to pass through it is _____.

8. to make clearer

DOWN

2. Something that allows light to pass through it is

_____ .

3. to bend light

5. the part of a telescope that focuses light

6. to bounce off a surface

Name _____

Unit Review

Visual Literacy

Sunny Scene

Study the picture below. How many different ways is light affecting or being affected by objects in the picture? Answer the questions below to describe what you see.

1. Which objects are **reflecting** light? Name at least two.

_____

2. Which objects are **absorbing** light? Name at least two.

_____

3. Which objects show light being **refracted**? Name two.

_____

4. What is the woman doing to protect herself from the sun's rays? Name at least two things.

_____

Name _____

Unit Review

Hands-on Activity

Liquid Lens

Daily Science

Big Idea 5

WEEK 5

You can use water's ability to refract light to make your own liquid magnifying glass!

What You Need

- sealable plastic bag
- tape
- water
- small objects (to study through the magnifying bag)

1. Fill the plastic bag two-thirds full with water.

2. Seal the bag, leaving it open at the corner just enough to squeeze all the air out of the top. Then seal the bag the rest of the way.

3. Fold over the sealed top of the bag so that the water is tightly contained. Tape the top down. This will keep the bag from leaking water.

4. Test your "magnifying glass" by placing it over the words on this page. Then test it with other objects.

What Did You Discover?

1. Describe what you saw through the bag. How did the objects look?

_____

2. How do you think the bag works? What role does **refraction** play?

_____

3. What do you think would happen if you added food coloring to the water? How might it change what you see through the bag?

_____

Big Idea 6

Electricity can exist as static electricity or travel as a current through a conductor.

Key Concepts
Static Electricity, Electric Current, and Circuits

National Standard
Electricity in circuits can produce light, heat, sound, and magnetic effects. Electrical circuits require a complete loop through which an electrical current can pass.

By third grade, students usually have a basic understanding of electricity, but they may not see it as a form of energy. In this unit, students will learn the difference between static electricity and electric current, and will also explore the following concepts:

→ electricity is a form of energy that can be converted to other forms of energy;

→ electricity can be observed as static electricity or as an electric current;

→ batteries can create electric energy; and

→ electric circuits and switches help control the flow of electricity.

Teacher Background

Electricity is a form of energy that can be converted into other forms of energy, such as light, heat, or mechanical energy. Electricity is observed in two states, either as static electricity or as an electric current.

Static electricity results from the buildup of electrons. Atoms gaining electrons gain a negative charge, and when these electrons discharge, it creates a spark. The spark can be as small as the shock you get when you touch a metal doorknob or as powerful as a bolt of lightning.

Electric current is the form of electricity that powers the appliances and devices we use. Electric current flows in a circuit, which must have a source of power, a conductor, and something to use the electricity. When a switch is added to a circuit, the switch can allow or stop the flow of electric current through the circuit.

Most electric current is generated in power stations, but portable devices such as cellular phones and flashlights require batteries. Batteries use chemical reactions to create electric current, which flows when the battery is integrated into a circuit.

For specific background information on each week's concepts, refer to the notes on pp. 158, 164, 170, and 176.

Unit Overview

WEEK 1: Where does lightning come from?

Connection to the Big Idea: Lightning is a form of static electricity.

Students learn that electricity is a form of energy. They discover that atoms have electrons that can build up and create a negative charge that, when discharged, creates static electricity, such as lightning. Finally, students learn that the electric shock they get when they touch metal is also static electricity.

Content Vocabulary: *atom, charge, electricity, electron, proton, static electricity*

WEEK 2: Why do electrical cords have metal plugs?

Connection to the Big Idea: Metals are ideal conductors of electric current.

Students learn that electricity can flow in a current, which is different from static electricity. They learn what conductors and insulators are and how these materials allow or impede the flow of electric current. Finally, students learn how power stations use conductors to send electricity to buildings.

Content Vocabulary: *appliance, conductor, current, insulator*

WEEK 3: How does flipping a switch light up a light bulb?

Connection to the Big Idea: Electric circuits allow us to use electric current.

Students begin by learning that electric current needs a circuit in order to flow, and a circuit consists of a power source, a conductor, and a device that uses the electricity. Students then discover that a switch allows or interrupts the flow of electricity through a current, and that when electric current flows into a light bulb, the bulb converts electrical energy into light.

Content Vocabulary: *circuit, outlet, source, switch*

WEEK 4: How does a battery make electricity?

Connection to the Big Idea: Batteries create electrical energy.

Students first learn that batteries are sources of electrical energy. Students then discover what is inside a battery and how current flows when a battery is part of a circuit. Finally, students learn that some batteries can be recharged.

Content Vocabulary: *battery, recharge*

WEEK 5: Unit Review

You may choose to do these activities to review concepts of electricity.

p. 182: Comprehension Students answer multiple-choice questions about key concepts from the unit.

p. 183: Vocabulary Students use key vocabulary from the unit to complete paragraphs.

p. 184: Visual Literacy Students use pictures to complete captions and correctly sequence how electricity travels from a power station.

p. 185: Hands-on Activity Students use static electricity to move metal cans. Materials and instructions are listed on the student page.

Big Idea 6

Electricity can exist as static electricity or travel as a current through a conductor.

Week 1

Where does lightning come from?

This week, students learn that lightning is a dramatic example of static electricity caused by atoms in storm clouds gaining and losing electrons. Atoms that gain electrons gain a negative charge, which then discharges in a spark of electricity that we see as lightning. The shock you sometimes get when you touch metal is also an example of static electricity. The strength of the shock is actually quite strong, but since it is so brief, it is only annoying, not dangerous.

Day One Vocabulary: *electricity*	Distribute page 159 and introduce the vocabulary word. Have volunteers read the introduction aloud. Then have students complete activity A. Invite volunteers to share their responses. Then have students complete activity B independently. For activity C, pair students or complete the activity as a group, if needed. Review the answers together.
Day Two Vocabulary: *atom, electron, proton*	Distribute page 160, introduce the vocabulary, and have volunteers read the introduction aloud. Use the diagram on the page to point out how protons and electrons are often represented by plus and minus signs. Then have students complete the activities independently. Review the answers together.
Day Three Vocabulary: *charge, static electricity*	Distribute page 161 and introduce the vocabulary. Then have volunteers read the introduction aloud. Confirm students' understanding of how something gains or loses a charge before having them complete the activities. Review the answers together.
Day Four	Activate prior knowledge by asking students if they have ever gotten a shock when they touched something metal. Distribute page 162 and have volunteers read the introduction aloud. Then have students complete the activities. Invite volunteers to share their responses to activity B.
Day Five	Tell students they will review everything they have learned about lightning and static electricity. Have them complete page 163. Go over the answers together.

Name _____

Day 1

Weekly Question

Where does lightning come from?

When you think of **electricity**, you might picture a lamp lighting up or a television turning on. But electricity isn't just in your home. If you have ever seen lightning flash across the sky, you have seen electricity in nature.

Lightning is a giant spark of energy. It can happen inside clouds or between clouds. It can also happen between a cloud and the ground. Lightning is a very powerful form of energy.

Vocabulary

electricity
a type of energy

A. Name three things that use electricity in your home.

1. _____ 2. _____ 3. _____

B. Write **true** or **false**.

1. Lightning can happen only between a cloud and the ground. _____

2. Electricity is a form of energy. _____

3. Lightning is not as powerful as light from a lamp. _____

C. Every second, there are about 100 lightning flashes on Earth! Eighty of these occur between clouds. Twenty occur between clouds and the ground. Use this information to answer the questions.

1. How many flashes occur in three seconds? _____

2. Every second, how many more flashes occur between clouds than between clouds and the ground? _____

Name _____

Day 2 *Weekly Question*
Where does lightning come from?

Electricity comes from **atoms**. Atoms are so small that you can't see them. And they are made up of even tinier parts called **protons** and **electrons**. Protons and electrons pull on each other. Sometimes the electrons will move from one atom to another.

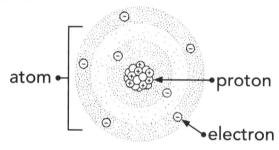

atom • proton • electron

A. Use vocabulary words to complete the sentences.

1. _____ have protons and electrons.

2. Electrons pull on _____.

3. Sometimes _____ from one atom will jump to another atom.

B. Check the box next to the words that complete each sentence.

1. Protons are found _____ atoms.

☐ in the middle of   ☐ spinning around   ☐ next to

2. Electrons are _____ atoms.

☐ bigger than   ☐ smaller than   ☐ the same size as

Vocabulary

atom
the smallest whole piece of matter

electron
a part of an atom that is the opposite of a proton

proton
a part of an atom that is the opposite of an electron

Name _____

Day 3

Weekly Question
Where does lightning come from?

Lightning occurs when the atoms in water droplets, dust, and bits of ice inside storm clouds pass electrons between each other. Atoms that pick up extra electrons gain a negative **charge**. Atoms that lose electrons gain a positive charge. The atoms pull on one another. When the pull grows strong enough, many electrons jump between the atoms all at once. This causes a giant spark of **static electricity**. We see lightning!

A. Look at each water droplet. Count the number of protons and electrons in it. Then check the box next to **positive** or **negative** to tell what kind of charge the droplet has.

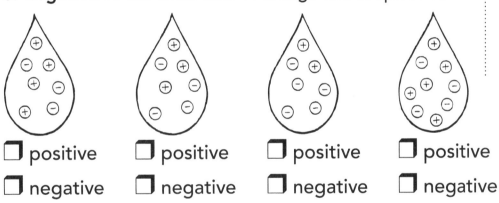

☐ positive   ☐ positive   ☐ positive   ☐ positive
☐ negative   ☐ negative   ☐ negative   ☐ negative

Vocabulary

charge
the state of having more or fewer electrons

static electricity
a form of energy that comes from the pull between protons and electrons

B. Write **true** or **false**.

1. Atoms trade protons when they are close together.   _____

2. An atom with a negative charge has more protons than electrons.   _____

3. Static electricity forms when many electrons jump between atoms all at once.   _____

4. Water, dust, and ice are made up of atoms.   _____

Name _____

Day 4

Weekly Question

Where does lightning come from?

Daily Science

Big Idea 6

WEEK 1

All static electricity comes from the buildup of electrons in one place. But it doesn't always produce giant bolts of lightning. Have you ever touched a doorknob and received a shock? When you walk across carpet or sit on a couch or chair, you pick up electrons. You build up a negative charge! Then when you touch a doorknob, the electrons jump from your hand to the knob. This creates a shock and a spark, just like a tiny lightning bolt.

A. Answer each question.

1. What kind of electricity gives you a shock when you

   touch a metal doorknob? _____

2. What part of an atom do you pick up from walking

   across carpet? _____

B. Draw a picture that shows how electrons travel from the carpet, through your body, and to a doorknob, producing a spark. Then write a caption below the picture to explain it.

Name _____

Day 5

Weekly Question

Where does lightning come from?

Daily Science

Big Idea 6

WEEK 1

A. Use the words in the box to complete the paragraph.

> charge   protons   electrons   static

Sari's class is studying electricity. Today she learned that

lightning is an example of _____ electricity,

which occurs when parts of an atom called _____

and _____ pull on each other. These parts have

an opposite _____.

B. Write **true** or **false**.

1. Thunder and lightning make atoms. _____

2. Atoms have protons and electrons. _____

3. Lightning is a giant spark of static electricity. _____

C. Label the diagram below. Write **atom**, **electron**, and **proton**.

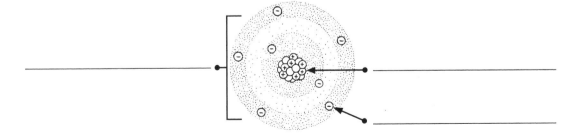

_____

Electricity can exist as static electricity or travel as a current through a conductor.

Week 2
Why do electrical cords have metal plugs?

This week, students learn the differences between static electricity and electric current, as well as the role that conductors and insulators play in how electricity travels. Unlike static electricity, an electric current is not a single discharge; it is always flowing. The metal plug of a power cord is a conductor that is connected to other metal wires wrapped in the plastic or rubber coating. The coating insulates the wires, so as electricity flows through them, it is impeded by the surrounding insulators. This week's lesson offers several opportunities to talk about safety issues, such as not sticking objects other than plugs into electrical outlets and keeping away from downed power lines.

Day One

Vocabulary: *appliance, current*

Distribute page 165. Introduce the vocabulary by asking students to think of some appliances they have seen or used and then think of things that move in a current. (water, air) Then have volunteers read the introduction aloud. Have students complete the activities, and then review the answers together.

Day Two

Vocabulary: *conductor*

Distribute page 166 and introduce the vocabulary word. Have volunteers read the introduction aloud. Then direct students to complete the activities independently. Invite volunteers to read their completed sentences for activity B aloud.

Day Three

Vocabulary: *insulator*

Materials: electrical wire

Distribute page 167 and introduce the vocabulary word. Show students the wire and explain that the metal part is a conductor and that the rubber coating is an insulator. Ask students to predict what might happen if the wire didn't have the rubber coating around it. (You might get shocked if it was used to conduct electricity.) Have volunteers read the introduction aloud. Then have students complete the activities. Invite volunteers to share their responses and explain their thinking for activity B.

Day Four

Distribute page 168 and have volunteers read the introduction aloud. Have a volunteer read the labels below the picture and explain what the arrows show. (how electricity travels) Then direct students to complete the activities. Invite students to share their responses and explain their thinking for activity B.

Day Five

Tell students they will review what they have learned about conductors and insulators. Have them complete page 169. Go over the answers together.

Name _____

Day 1

Weekly Question

Why do electrical cords have metal plugs?

Remember that a lightning bolt is a giant spark in the sky. It is an example of static electricity. Another kind of electricity makes things such as lamps, televisions, and other **appliances** work. This kind of electricity flows in a **current**, similar to how the water in a river flows. The electric current in your home is always flowing. It doesn't just end with a spark, the way static electricity does.

Vocabulary

appliance
a machine that uses electricity

current
the flow of something

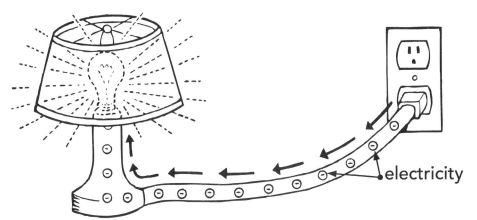

electricity

A. List four appliances in your house that use current electricity.

1. _____   3. _____

2. _____   4. _____

B. Complete each sentence. Write **electric current** or **static electricity**.

1. _____ is the continuing flow of electricity.

2. A lightning bolt is an example of _____.

3. Appliances need an _____ to work.

4. _____ ends in a spark of energy.

Name _____

Day 2

Weekly Question

Why do electrical cords have metal plugs?

Remember that electricity is the flow of electrons. Some materials allow electrons to flow through them easily. These materials are known as **conductors**. Metals such as copper, gold, and silver are good conductors. They allow electrons to flow through them easily. That's why electrical wires and plugs are made from metal.

Vocabulary

conductor
a material that allows electricity to flow through it

A. Write **true** or **false**.

1. Electricity flows easily through everything.   _____

2. Metals are good conductors.   _____

3. Electrical wires are made from electrons.   _____

4. Electrons pass easily through copper.   _____

B. Use the words in the box to complete the sentences.

> copper   plug   conducts

1. The lamp had a cord with a metal _____ at the end.

2. James used _____ wire to make a conductor.

3. A metal pole _____ electricity better than a wooden one.

Name _____

Day 3

Weekly Question

Why do electrical cords have metal plugs?

When an electrical appliance is switched on, electricity flows into the plug of the appliance's cord. Then it flows through the cord's wires to make the appliance work.

So why don't we get a shock from touching the cord? The electrical wires are wrapped in rubber, which is an **insulator**. Insulators are materials that do not let electrons flow through them easily. Rubber, plastic, wood, and glass are good insulators.

Vocabulary

insulator
a material that does not allow electricity to flow through it

A. Look at the items below. Write whether each one is a **conductor** or an **insulator**.

copper wire

rubber ball

plastic straw

_____   _____   _____

glass bowl

steel spring

_____   _____

B. People who work on power lines always wear thick gloves and boots with thick soles. Why do you think that is? Explain how the gloves and boots protect the workers.

_____

Name _____

Weekly Question
Why do electrical cords have metal plugs?

The electricity in your home comes from power stations in the city or town where you live. It travels through giant wires that are buried underground or attached to poles high above the ground. The wires are made of metal.

Sometimes, during storms or accidents, these wires will fall to the ground. If you ever see a fallen power line, stay far away from it! Your body is a good conductor, so electricity from the wires could flow through you and injure you.

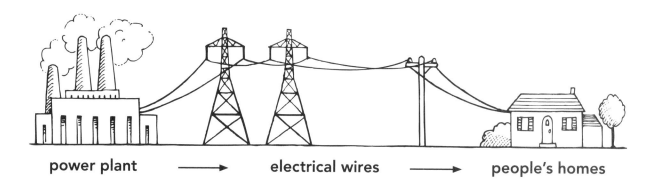

power plant → electrical wires → people's homes

A. Write **true** or **false**.

   1. Electrical wires that are not covered can be dangerous. _____

   2. Power stations use giant wires to conduct electricity. _____

   3. Your house makes its own electricity. _____

B. Ocean water is a better conductor than fresh water is. Your skin isn't the best conductor, but your blood, which contains water and salt, is better. What do you think the "secret ingredient" is that makes ocean water and blood good conductors?

_____

Name _____

Day 5

Weekly Question

Why do electrical cords have metal plugs?

A. Use the words in the box to complete the paragraph.

> appliance   insulator   current   conductor

Every day, you probably use an _____ that gets

electricity from a plug in the wall. The plug is attached to a wire

_____, which has an electric _____

flowing through it. The wire is coated with an _____

that keeps you from getting a shock.

B. Write **true** or **false**.

1. A conductor allows an electric current to flow.   _____

2. Rubber is a better conductor than copper is.   _____

3. A cord that is missing some rubber is dangerous.   _____

C. Describe each item below. Write **conductor** or **insulator**.

1. copper wire   _____

2. plastic sheet   _____

3. rubber cord   _____

4. metal tool   _____

Daily Science
Big Idea 6

Electricity can exist as static electricity or travel as a current through a conductor.

Week 3

How does flipping a switch light up a light bulb?

This week, students will learn about circuits, switches, and how light bulbs convert electrical energy into light and heat. Electric current requires a circuit to flow, and all circuits must be closed loops. The light switch on the wall completes or breaks the circuit, depending on whether the switch is on or off. When electricity makes contact with a light bulb, another switch is activated, and the bulb converts the electricity into light and sometimes into heat as well.

Day One

Vocabulary: *circuit, outlet*

Distribute page 171 and introduce the vocabulary. Develop *outlet* by explaining how the word can be used in relation to other things besides electricity. For example, ask: **What is a good outlet when you think something is funny?** (laughter) Invite volunteers to think of other good examples of outlets for different things. Then have volunteers read the introduction aloud. Have students complete the activities. Invite volunteers to share their responses and explain their thinking for activity B.

Day Two

Vocabulary: *source*

Distribute page 172 and introduce the vocabulary word. Have volunteers read the introduction aloud. Then have students complete the activities independently. Invite volunteers to share their responses and explain their thinking for activity B.

Day Three

Vocabulary: *switch*

Distribute page 173 and introduce the vocabulary word. Have volunteers read the introduction aloud, and then invite students to name other kinds of switches. Have students complete the activities. Invite volunteers to share their answers and explain their thinking for activity B.

Day Four

Materials: different kinds of bulbs (optional)

Distribute page 174 and have volunteers read the introduction aloud. If you brought bulbs, show them to students. Have students complete activity A independently. For activity B, if you have the bulbs, consider letting students compare and contrast the different kinds of bulbs based on information in the paragraph and their own observations. Go over the answers together.

Day Five

Tell students they will review what they learned about circuits and switches. Have them complete page 175. Go over the answers together.

Name _____

Day 1

Weekly Question

How does flipping a switch light up a light bulb?

You know that electricity needs a conductor to flow. It must also have a path. This path is called a **circuit**. A circuit is a loop. Electricity won't flow unless the loop is complete. This means that when you plug a lamp into an outlet in the wall, you complete the circuit. Electricity flows to the lamp and then back to the **outlet**.

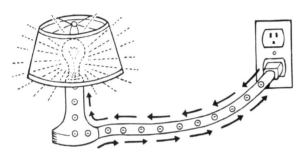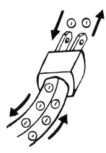

Vocabulary

circuit
a loop or path along which an electrical current flows

outlet
a place in the wall where you can plug in devices that use electricity

A. Circle the word or words that complete each sentence.

1. The path that electricity flows in is a _____.

   cord   circuit   conductor

2. For electricity to flow, a circuit must be _____.

   complete   in the wall   near a lamp

3. When electricity flows in a circuit, it flows in _____.

   one direction   two directions

B. Which one is more like a circuit, a race track or a maze? Explain your answer.

_____

Name _____

Weekly Question

Day 2

How does flipping a switch light up a light bulb?

All circuits have a source, a conductor, and a device that uses the electricity. Look at the circuit below. The wires are conductors that allow the electric current to flow from the battery, which is the **source**, to the bulb. When the circuit is complete, the bulb lights up.

Vocabulary

source
a thing that produces electricity

A. Write **true** or **false**.

1. If Lisa removes one of the wires, the bulb will still shine.

_____

2. If Gary replaces the battery, the bulb will still shine.

_____

3. If Sarah replaces the bulb with an electric clock, the circuit will still be complete.

_____

B. If power stations send electric current to your house, are they using circuits? Explain your answer.

_____

_____

Day 3

How does flipping a switch light up a light bulb?

Daily Science

Big Idea 6

WEEK 3

Many circuits don't need an electric current flowing through them all the time. To save electricity, they have a **switch**. The switch turns the supply of electricity on and off. When you flip a switch on, you complete the circuit that allows electric current to flow. When you flip the switch off, you break the circuit. The electric current stops flowing.

Switches come in many different forms. The on/off button on a computer and the knob on an electric stove are switches, just like the light switch on a wall.

Vocabulary

switch
a part of an electrical circuit that stops electricity or allows it to flow

A. Check the box next to the circuit that is turned on. Circle the switch.

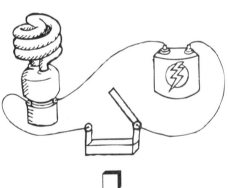
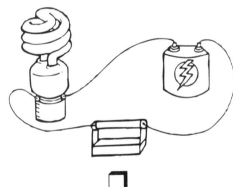

B. Answer the questions.

1. Some electrical devices, such as smoke detectors and refrigerators, don't have a switch. Why might that be?

_____

2. When you pause a video game instead of turning it off, are you breaking a circuit? Explain your answer.

_____

Name _____

Weekly Question

Day 4

How does flipping a switch light up a light bulb?

You know that when an electrical current flows into a light bulb, it lights up. But where does the light come from? Electrical energy can be turned into other types of energy, including light and heat. When electric current reaches a tiny piece of metal inside some light bulbs, the metal gets very hot. It starts to glow and produce light. Other bulbs have a special gas inside of them. When electricity reaches the gas, the gas changes the electrical energy into light.

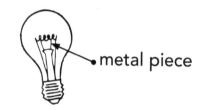
metal piece

incandescent bulb

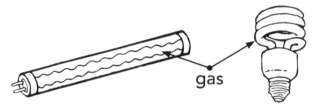
gas

fluorescent bulbs

A. Use the words in the box to complete the paragraph.

In 1800, Humphry Davy discovered how to use

_____ to create light. Then, in 1879,

Thomas Edison invented the first _____.

It had a tiny piece of metal that turned electricity into

_____ and _____.

> light bulb
>
> heat
>
> electricity
>
> light

B. Compare and contrast an incandescent bulb with a fluorescent bulb. Name one way they are alike and one way they are different.

_____

Name _____

Weekly Question

Day 5

How does flipping a switch light up a light bulb?

A. Look at the diagram. Label the **source**, **conductor**, **switch**, and **bulb**. Then write a caption to explain what the diagram shows. Use the word **circuit** in your caption.

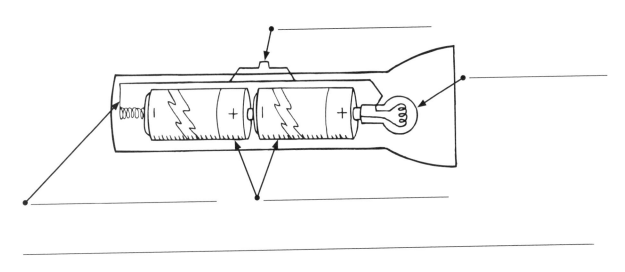

_____

_____

_____

B. Number the steps below in the correct order to show how a lamp in your home lights up.

____ The light bulb lights up.

____ Gas or a tiny strip of metal inside the bulb changes electrical energy into light.

____ The power station creates the electricity.

____ Flipping a switch in your home completes the circuit to send electricity from the wires to the light bulb.

____ Wires carry electricity from the power station to your home.

Big Idea 6

Electricity can exist as static electricity or travel as a current through a conductor.

Week 4

How does a battery make electricity?

This week, students will learn about batteries. Batteries convert chemical energy into electrical energy. When a battery is connected to a circuit, chemicals inside the battery react to release electrons, which flow through the rod inside the battery and through the circuit. After a while, many batteries are incapable of producing more chemical reactions to release electrons. But some batteries can be recharged, and they are capable of producing electricity many more times.

Day One Vocabulary: *battery* Materials: batteries of various sizes (optional)	Activate prior knowledge by asking students to describe what batteries are and what they do. If you have them, show students the batteries you brought. Distribute page 177 and introduce the vocabulary word. Have volunteers read the introduction aloud. Then have students complete activities A and B independently. For the oral activity, consider pairing students or completing the activity as a group.
Day Two	Distribute page 178 and have volunteers read the introduction aloud. Activate prior knowledge by reviewing what happens when an atom gains electrons. (It builds up a negative charge.) Point out the diagram of the battery and explain that the negative side of a battery is where the electrons build up. Explain that a battery produces an electric current, not static electricity, but scientists use the same terms, *positive* and *negative*, to talk about electricity. Direct students to complete the activities.
Day Three Materials: flashlight with batteries	Distribute page 179 and have volunteers read the introduction aloud. If you have it, show students the flashlight. Demonstrate putting the batteries in the flashlight incorrectly and ask students to surmise why the flashlight doesn't work. (The circuit isn't correct and the electric current cannot flow.) Then have students complete the activities. Invite volunteers to share their responses and explain their thinking for activity B.
Day Four Vocabulary: *recharge*	Distribute page 180 and introduce the vocabulary word. Develop *recharge* by explaining that the prefix *re-* means to do something again. Have volunteers read the introduction aloud. Then have students complete the activities. Invite volunteers to share their responses and explain their thinking for activity B.
Day Five	Tell students they will review what they have learned about batteries. Have them complete page 181. Go over the answers together.

Name _____

Day 1

Weekly Question

How does a battery make electricity?

A **battery** makes an electric current, just as a power station does. Batteries come in many shapes and sizes. Some batteries, such as those found in watches or hearing aids, are very small. Other batteries are very large. The world's largest battery is in Fairbanks, Alaska. It is the size of a football field!

Vocabulary

battery
a device that uses chemicals to make an electric current

A. Write **true** or **false**.

1. A battery makes an electric current. _____

2. Batteries come in only one size. _____

3. Large batteries make static electricity. _____

B. Look at the different batteries. Think about their sizes and shapes to help you match the batteries with the things they go in.

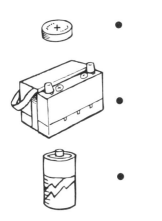

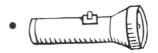

 Talk

A smoke detector gets electricity from the wires in your home, but it also has a battery. Why is that? Discuss it with a partner.

Name _____

Day 2

Weekly Question

How does a battery make electricity?

A battery has two ends, usually called "positive" and "negative." Inside the battery there is a liquid or a paste. The chemicals in the paste create electricity. The rod in the battery conducts electrons from the negative end to the positive end. But the electrons won't flow through the rod unless the positive and negative ends of the battery are connected to a circuit.

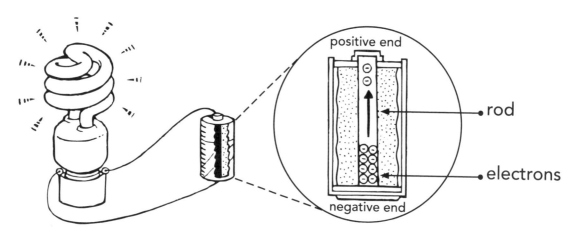

A. Write the word that completes each sentence.

   1. On a battery, the _____ end is opposite the negative end.

   2. The paste inside a battery creates _____.

   3. The electricity inside a battery can flow only if both ends

   are connected to a _____.

B. Write three things you've used recently that have batteries.

   1. _____   **2.** _____   **3.** _____

Name _____

Weekly Question

Day 3

How does a battery make electricity?

Remember that a circuit needs both a source and a conductor in order for electricity to flow. Inside a flashlight there are wires, or conductors, that carry electricity to the light bulb. The battery is the electrical source. When the positive and negative ends of the battery are connected to the wires, they complete the circuit. The battery creates an electric current that flows to the bulb, and the flashlight shines!

A. Look at the diagram below. Label the **source**, the **conductor**, and the **bulb**. Then read each question and check the box next to the correct answer.

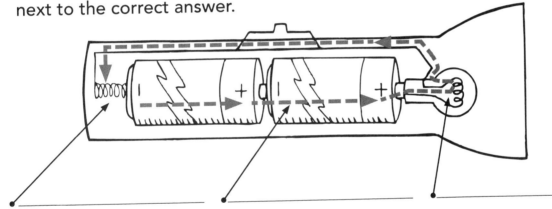

1. Which way does electricity flow through the battery to the bulb?

   ☐ from negative to positive   ☐ from positive to negative

2. Which of these creates electricity?

   ☐ the switch   ☐ the light bulb   ☐ the battery

B. Why does it make more sense for a flashlight to have a battery than a cord that plugs into a wall? Explain your answer.

_____

Name _____

Weekly Question

How does a battery make electricity?

Daily Science

Big Idea 6

WEEK 4

The chemical paste in many batteries stops making electricity after a while. But some batteries can be **recharged**. When electricity moves back into the battery, it changes the battery's chemicals so that they can make their own electricity again.

One kind of battery that can be recharged is a car battery. A part in the car recharges the battery while the car runs. Other batteries can be recharged by using a tool called a charger. The charger plugs into an electrical outlet in your home. Electricity flows through the charger and into the battery.

Vocabulary

recharge
to charge again

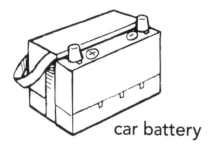
car battery

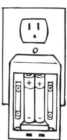
battery charger

A. Write **true** or **false**.

1. All batteries can be recharged. _____

2. Some batteries use the electricity in your home to recharge. _____

3. Rechargeable batteries have chemicals in them. _____

B. Telephones, music players, laptop computers, and many cameras use rechargeable batteries. Explain why using them in these devices might be better than using regular batteries.

_____

Name _____

Day 5

Weekly Question
How does a battery make electricity?

A. Use words from the box to complete the sentences.

> battery   negative   positive   recharged

1. A _____ has chemicals that create electricity.

2. Car batteries can be _____.

3. Batteries have a _____ and a _____ end.

B. Circle the electrical source for this circuit. Then draw arrows to show which way the electricity is flowing.

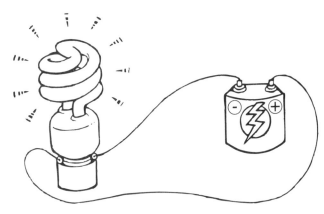

C. Write **true** or **false**.

1. A battery makes static electricity.   _____

2. All batteries can be recharged.   _____

3. In circuits, batteries are the electrical source.   _____

4. In batteries, electricity flows from the negative end to the positive end.   _____

Name _____

 Unit Review

Comprehension

All About Electricity

Fill in the bubble next to the correct answer.

1. Electricity moves through a path called _____.

   Ⓐ a source

   Ⓑ static electricity

   Ⓒ a circuit

   Ⓓ an electron

2. A circuit needs _____ to be complete.

   Ⓐ a source

   Ⓑ a conductor

   Ⓒ a closed path

   Ⓓ all of these

3. The _____ inside a flashlight makes electricity.

   Ⓐ battery

   Ⓑ conductor

   Ⓒ light bulb

   Ⓓ insulator

4. Rubber is an example of _____.

   Ⓐ a conductor

   Ⓑ an insulator

   Ⓒ a circuit

   Ⓓ a switch

5. Lightning is an example of _____.

   Ⓐ an electric current

   Ⓑ protons

   Ⓒ static electricity

   Ⓓ a conductor

6. The parts of an atom with a negative charge are _____.

   Ⓐ electrons

   Ⓑ switches

   Ⓒ protons

   Ⓓ lightning

Name _____

Recharge your vocabulary! Use words from the boxes to complete the paragraphs.

Lightning is a giant spark of _____

electricity. It is made when _____ gain

or lose electrons and build up positive and negative

_____. Static electricity is different from

electricity that flows in a _____. This kind

of electricity flows through metal wires and other

_____.

| current |
| static |
| charges |
| conductors |
| atoms |
| insulator |

Do you know how a flashlight works? Flashlights use

batteries, which are _____ of electricity

that are easy to carry. Electricity from the _____

flows through wires to the light bulb in a path called a

_____. The button on a flashlight is a

_____. It completes or breaks the circuit,

turning the flashlight on and off.

| batteries |
| switch |
| outlets |
| sources |
| electrons |
| circuit |

Name _____

Look at the pictures. Complete a caption for each one, using a phrase from the box. Then number the pictures in the correct order to show how electricity travels.

- huge amounts of electrical energy
- insulated cord to the computer
- carry electricity to the outlets
- from the power plant to a house

How Electricity Travels

☐ Wires in the walls _____

_____ .

☐ A power plant uses machines to make _____

_____ .

☐ Electricity flows through the _____

_____ .

☐ Power lines carry electrical energy _____

_____ .

Name _____

Hands-on Activity

Charged-up Relay

You know that static electricity is a pull between atoms. Now use that pull to win a race! The object of the race is to roll an empty soda can across the finish line without touching the balloon to the can!

What You Need

- large, open space with a flat surface
- at least 2 teams of 5 players
- inflated balloons for each team
- one empty metal soda or juice can for each team

1. Set up a starting line and a finish line. Place the empty can on its side at the starting line. Have the first person on each team "charge up" the balloon by rubbing it on his or her clothes.

2. At the signal, the first person on each team uses the balloon to pull the can across the finish line. However, if the balloon touches the can, the player must return to the starting line and start over. If the balloon loses its charge at any time, the player should rub it to charge it again.

3. When the player reaches the finish line, he or she picks up the can and runs back to the start. The next team member repeats the process. The first team to have the last player cross the finish line wins!

What Did You Discover?

1. What did you do to make the balloon gain electrons?

_____

2. What made the soda can roll? _____

_____

3. Who won the race? _____

Answer Key

Big Idea 1: *Week 1 • Day 1*

A. Any two of the following: size, color, scent
B. 1. reproduce   2. adaptation
C. Answers will vary—e.g., The golden poppy is bright orange. It smells very nice.

Big Idea 1: *Week 1 • Day 2*

A. 3, 1, 5, 4, 2
B. pollen, pollinates
TALK: Answers will vary— e.g., Wind carries pollen from one flower to another.

Big Idea 1: *Week 1 • Day 3*

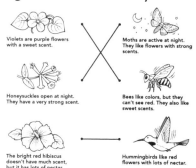

Big Idea 1: *Week 1 • Day 4*

A. 1. false   2. false   3. true
B. Answers will vary—e.g., The skunk uses bad smells to protect itself.

Big Idea 1: *Week 1 • Day 5*

A. 1. adaptations   3. pollen
   2. pollen
B. adaptations, pollen, survive
C. Flowers make pollen and attract animals to spread the pollen. Flowers also make seeds to help the plant reproduce.

Big Idea 1: *Week 2 • Day 1*

A.

	Dolphin	Human
Has arms and legs	no	yes
Breathes air	yes	yes
Needs regular sleep	yes	yes
Has a nose	no	yes

B. backbone
C. Answers will vary—e.g., warm bed, glass of milk, night light

Big Idea 1: *Week 2 • Day 2*

A. 1. The blowhole helps the dolphin breathe.
   2. The tail allows the dolphin to swim.
   3. The flippers help the dolphin steer.
B.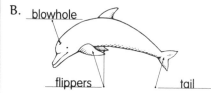

Big Idea 1: *Week 2 • Day 3*

A. 1. to control its blowhole
   2. to look out for danger
B. 1. false   2. true   3. false
C. A dolphin keeps swimming while it sleeps.

Big Idea 1: *Week 2 • Day 4*

A. 1. to breathe
   2. so that it can pump water through its gills
B. 1. swim   2. sleep
C. Answers will vary—e.g.,
   Same: They both keep swimming while sleeping.
   Different: A dolphin breathes through its blowhole, while a shark breathes through its gills.

Big Idea 1: *Week 2 • Day 5*

A.

B. mammals, blowhole, automatically, adaptation

Big Idea 1: *Week 3 • Day 1*

A. Any two of the following: little rain, very hot and dry, water evaporates quickly
B. 1. a kangaroo rat
   2. leaving it by the window on a warm, sunny day

Big Idea 1: *Week 3 • Day 2*

A. 1. leaves   2. water   3. sunlight
B. They would dry up and fall off.

Big Idea 1: *Week 3 • Day 3*

A. Animals spread the cactus around when it sticks to them.
B. The quills protect the porcupine.
C. 1. true   2. false

Big Idea 1: *Week 3 • Day 4*

A.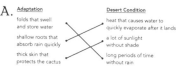
B.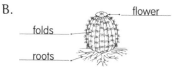

Big Idea 1: *Week 3 • Day 5*

A. Any two of the following: provide shade, direct water, protect the cactus, help it reproduce
B. survive, evaporate, spines, folds
C. **Spines** are to **cactus** as **leaves** are to **plant**.

Big Idea 1: *Week 4 • Day 1*

A. 1. true   2. false   3. false
B.

This is the ___route___ of the Arctic tern when it ___migrates___.

Big Idea 1: *Week 4 • Day 2*

A. 1. longer, warmer days
   2. Any two of the following: nectar, berries, seeds, and insects
   3. to find more food
B. Hummingbirds migrate to find new flowers. Hawks don't migrate because they will still have food.

Big Idea 1: *Week 4 • Day 3*

A. 1. better habitat for reproducing
2. fewer predators
3. longer days
B. 1. Song Sparrow
2. Louisiana
3. no

Big Idea 1: *Week 4 • Day 4*

1. They store a lot of fat to have enough energy for their trip.
2. Birds that don't migrate have different adaptations because they don't need to migrate.

TALK: Answers will vary.

Big Idea 1: *Week 4 • Day 5*

A. B
B. Any of the following: to find more food, their habitat changed, to be warmer
C. migrate, reproduce, habitat, predators

Big Idea 1: *Week 5 • Unit Review 1*

A. 1. C   2. B   3. B
B. 1. true   2. false   3. true

Big Idea 1: *Week 5 • Unit Review 2*

1. reproduce, pollen, adaptations
2. mammals, automatically, blowhole
3. folds, spines, evaporate
4. migrate, routes, habitats

Big Idea 1: *Week 5 • Unit Review 3*

1. They are traveling south, based on the dates on the map.
2. Mexico   3. 30 days

Big Idea 1: *Week 5 • Unit Review 4*

Answers will vary.

Big Idea 2: *Week 1 • Day 1*

A. F, V, V, F, V
B. 1. false   2. false   3. true

Big Idea 2: *Week 1 • Day 2*

A. 1. pollinated   2. seeds   3. fruit
B. Plants provide food for animals and the animals help distribute the seeds to grow.

Big Idea 2: *Week 1 • Day 3*

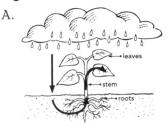

A.
Lettuce — Root
This green vegetable is used in salads. / This absorbs water from the soil.
Potato — Stem
This vegetable grows under the ground. / This connects the roots to the leaves.
Celery — Leaf
This vegetable grows above the ground. / This is usually flat and green and absorbs sunlight.

B. Answers will vary:
Vegetable—spinach
Plant part—leaf

Big Idea 2: *Week 1 • Day 4*

A. leaves, root, seed
B. 1. true   2. false   3. true
C. Answers will vary—e.g., tomato, apple, banana, spinach, etc.

Big Idea 2: *Week 1 • Day 5*

A. 1. pollinated   3. leaves, stem,
2. seeds   roots
B. fruit, vegetable, fruit, vegetable
C. C

Big Idea 2: *Week 2 • Day 1*

A.

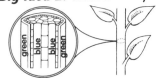

B. 1. roots   3. to grow
2. leaves   and survive

Big Idea 2: *Week 2 • Day 2*

A. 1. diffuse   2. tap   3. absorb
B. 1. diffuse   2. tap

Big Idea 2: *Week 2 • Day 3*

B. 1. nutrients, stem
2. protects, tubes
C. Answers will vary—e.g.,
1. food   2. vitamins

Big Idea 2: *Week 2 • Day 4*

A. 1. false   2. true   3. false
B. to keep the water in the leaves
TALK: Our pores let water out of our bodies like a leaf's pores do.

Big Idea 2: *Week 2 • Day 5*

A. 4, 1, 5, 2, 3
B. tap root, diffuse root
C. 1. true   2. true   3. false

Big Idea 2: *Week 3 • Day 1*

A.

B. 1. seed   2. distribute   3. flower

Big Idea 2: *Week 3 • Day 2*

A. 1. parachute   2. conditions
B. 1. false   2. true
C. Dandelions would grow farther apart because the wind blows the parachutes far away from the plant.

Big Idea 2: *Week 3 • Day 3*

A. 1. false   3. false   5. true
2. true   4. false
B. The seed coat protects the seed from drying out.

Big Idea 2: *Week 3 • Day 4*

1. water   3. animals
2. animals   4. wind

Big Idea 2: *Week 3 • Day 5*

A. distribute, conditions, seed coat
B. seed germ   seed coat   parachute
C. water, wind, animals

Big Idea 2: *Week 4 • Day 1*

A. green
B. 1. in the cells
2. chlorophyll, sunlight
3. It would not be green.

Big Idea 2: *Week 4 • Day 2*

A. 1. sunlight, photosynthesis
2. carbon dioxide, water
B. during the summer

Big Idea 2: *Week 4 • Day 3*

A. 2, 1, 3, 5, 4
B. There is more sunlight.

Big Idea 2: *Week 4 • Day 4*

A. 1. true   2. true
B. 1. warmer temperature
   2. more sunlight
   3. more water in the air
C. They are making more chlorophyll.

Big Idea 2: *Week 4 • Day 5*

A. 1. photosynthesis
   2. carbon dioxide
   3. chlorophyll
B. 1. false   3. false
   2. true   4. false
C. They have a lot of chlorophyll.

Big Idea 2: *Week 5 • Unit Review 1*

1. A   2. D   3. B   4. B   5. D   6. A

Big Idea 2: *Week 5 • Unit Review 2*

A.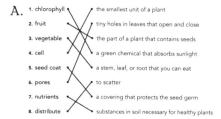
B. 1. pollen
   2. photosynthesis
   3. parachute

Big Idea 2: *Week 5 • Unit Review 3*

1. b   2. d   3. a   4. c

Big Idea 2: *Week 5 • Unit Review 4*

Answers will vary.

Big Idea 3: *Week 1 • Day 1*

A.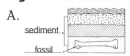
B. 1. false   2. true   3. false

Big Idea 3: *Week 1 • Day 2*

A. dinosaur bone
B. 1. minerals
   2. rock
   3. No, it doesn't contain bones.

Big Idea 3: *Week 1 • Day 3*

A. a leaf, a tooth
B. 1. They help scientists learn how animals behaved or moved.
   2. A mold is more common because it does not require an animal to have bones or other hard parts.

Big Idea 3: *Week 1 • Day 4*

A. 2, 3, 1
B. 1. amber   2. resin
C. what the animal looked like

Big Idea 3: *Week 1 • Day 5*

A. cast, amber, mold, trace
B. 1. false   2. true   3. true
C. 3, 1, 2

Big Idea 3: *Week 2 • Day 1*

1. sandstone, limestone (or shale)
2. They turn into rock.
3. There are no plants or animals inside Earth where the granite is formed.

Big Idea 3: *Week 2 • Day 2*

A.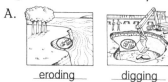
eroding   digging
B. 1. true   2. false   3. false

Big Idea 3: *Week 2 • Day 3*

1. sandstone
2. Answers will vary—e.g., worms, sea lilies, mollusk shells
3. shale

Big Idea 3: *Week 2 • Day 4*

A.
B. 1. false   2. true   3. true

Big Idea 3: *Week 2 • Day 5*

A. fossil, sediment, preserve, paleontologists, erode
B. Any two of the following: limestone, sandstone, or shale
C. 1. false   3. false
   2. true   4. false

Big Idea 3: *Week 3 • Day 1*

1. bottom layer because that layer was buried first
2. older than 2 million years because the bottom layer would be even older
3. so they can better understand Earth

Big Idea 3: *Week 3 • Day 2*

1. true   2. false   3. false   4. false
TALK: Scientist know more about 65 million years ago because it is more recent, and more of those fossils are easier to discover because they are above the older fossils.

Big Idea 3: *Week 3 • Day 3*

A. 1. million   2. age   3. ocean
B. Answers will vary—e.g., cockroaches because there are so many of them

Big Idea 3: *Week 3 • Day 4*

A. 1. when different plants and animals lived
   2. dinosaur fossils
   3. No, because trilobites were extinct about 100 million years before the dinosaurs.
B.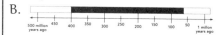

Big Idea 3: *Week 3 • Day 5*

A. fossil record, trilobite, marker fossil
B. 1. 200   3. 3
   2. 400   4. 65

Big Idea 3: *Week 4 • Day 1*

A. 4 2
   1 3
B. 1. It was very hot.
   2. Life probably began in the ocean.

Big Idea 3: *Week 4 • Day 2*

1. crust   3. crust
2. mantle   4. mantle
TALK: The crust would move less because the mantle would move less.

Big Idea 3: *Week 4 • Day 3*

A. 2, 3, 1
B. Mountains, continents

Big Idea 3: *Week 4 • Day 4*

A.

B. 1. false   2. true   3. true

Big Idea 3: *Week 4 • Day 5*

A. 1. A   2. B   3. D   4. A
B. The fossils would be older than 250 million years because that is when the landmass split into two continents.

Big Idea 3: *Week 5 • Unit Review 1*

1. A   3. B   5. B
2. C   4. D   6. B

Big Idea 3: *Week 5 • Unit Review 2*

1. hard   6. fossils
2. fossil   7. nonliving
3. trace fossil 8. mantle
4. fossil   9. keep it
5. layers of rock 10. go away

Big Idea 3: *Week 5 • Unit Review 3*

1. c   2. a   3. d   4. b

Big Idea 3: *Week 5 • Unit Review 4*

1. mold
2. so they don't damage the fossils
3. Answers will vary.

Big Idea 4: *Week 1 • Day 1*

A. 1. B   2. C
B. Answers will vary—e.g.,
   1. You can feel the wind blowing.
   2. You can smell different things in the air.

Big Idea 4: *Week 1 • Day 2*

A. 1. A   2. B   3. low
B. 1. true   2. true   3. false

Big Idea 4: *Week 1 • Day 3*

1. New York   3. Flagstaff
2. Flagstaff   4. New York
TALK: Answers will vary.

Big Idea 4: *Week 1 • Day 4*

A.

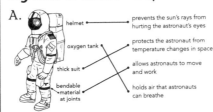

B. Answers will vary—e.g., There is no oxygen in outer space and we need oxygen to breathe.

Big Idea 4: *Week 1 • Day 5*

A. 1. oxygen   3. atmosphere
   2. sea level   4. altitude
B. 1. false   3. true
   2. false   4. true
C. There is probably more air near Miami because it is closer to sea level.

Big Idea 4: *Week 2 • Day 1*

A. 1. carbon dioxide
   2. dissolves
B. 1. water, carbon dioxide
   2. Gas is escaping from the can.

Big Idea 4: *Week 2 • Day 2*

A. lowest, highest
B. 1. up   2. full

Big Idea 4: *Week 2 • Day 3*

A. the balloon gets smaller
B. 1. false   2. true
TALK: All the gas in the soda escapes.

Big Idea 4: *Week 2 • Day 4*

A. Answers will vary—e.g.,
   1. spray paint   2. basketball
B. Answers will vary.

Big Idea 4: *Week 2 • Day 5*

A. 1. dissolved
   2. carbon dioxide
   3. air pressure
B. 1. false   2. true   3. true
C. There is more pressure at the beach because gravity is stronger at sea level.

Big Idea 4: *Week 3 • Day 1*

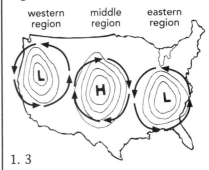

western region   middle region   eastern region

1. 3
2. middle region
3. counterclockwise

Big Idea 4: *Week 3 • Day 2*

1. The sun heats the air. Warm air rises and circulates.
2. It weighs less.
3. There is less pressure.
TALK: There is no cool air to make the warm air circulate.

Big Idea 4: *Week 3 • Day 3*

1. wind vane   3. anemometer
2. anemometer   4. wind vane

Big Idea 4: *Week 3 • Day 4*

1. true   3. true
2. false   4. true
TALK: Answers will vary.

Big Idea 4: *Week 3 • Day 5*

A. 1. Meteorologists
   2. circulates
   3. anemometers
   4. Wind vanes
   5. pressure systems
B.
cool air ⬇ ↻ ⬆ warm air

C. 1. false   2. true   3. true

Big Idea 4: *Week 4 • Day 1*

A. wings covered with feathers; strong muscles; hollow bones
B. 1. false   2. true   3. false

Big Idea 4: *Week 4 • Day 2*

1. over   3. thrust
2. under   4. water

Big Idea 4: Week 4 • Day 3

A. 1. true   3. true
    2. false   4. true
B. A glider uses wind and thermal currents to remain in flight.

Big Idea 4: Week 4 • Day 4

Bird	What It Does	Type of Wings
Canada Goose	migrates a great distance from Canada to southern United States	long
Sparrow	darts from perch to perch and does not migrate	short
Albatross	travels long distances, gliding on ocean winds	long
Wren	flits from bush to bush, trying to catch insects	short

Big Idea 4: Week 4 • Day 5

A. 1. thermal   4. thrust
    2. lift   5. adaptation
    3. drag
B. 1. false   2. false   3. true
C.

Big Idea 4: Week 5 • Unit Review 1

1. B   2. A   3. B   4. D   5. D

Big Idea 4: Week 5 • Unit Review 2

1. how high   8. valley
2. fly   9. fly
3. mixed into   10. close to Earth
4. weather   11. low
5. anemometer   12. gases
6. thrust   13. feathers
7. circle   14. air

Big Idea 4: Week 5 • Unit Review 3

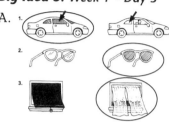

Big Idea 4: Week 5 • Unit Review 4

1. It swirls like a tornado.
2. Both have circulation.

Big Idea 5: Week 1 • Day 1

A. 1. true   2. true   3. false
B. energy, radiate, ray, sunlight

Big Idea 5: Week 1 • Day 2

A. 1. transparent   3. opaque
    2. opaque   4. transparent
B. 4, 3, 1, 2

Big Idea 5: Week 1 • Day 3

A.

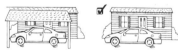

B. 1. tinted because the bus would stay cooler
    2. translucent because you couldn't see with opaque lenses

Big Idea 5: Week 1 • Day 4

A. 1. The light passes through the walls of the greenhouse.
    2. The air in the greenhouse warms up.
    3. Tomatoes growing in the greenhouse get ripe.
B. Translucent walls block more light. Translucent walls would be better when you need less light or heat in the greenhouse.

Big Idea 5: Week 1 • Day 5

A. translucent, transparent, opaque
B. 1. transparent   4. translucent
    2. opaque   5. ray
    3. absorb
C.

Big Idea 5: Week 2 • Day 1

A. 1. B
    2. A; It doesn't change its path because it does not pass through water.
B. 1. B   2. C

Big Idea 5: Week 2 • Day 2

A.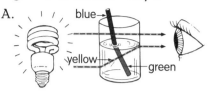

B. 1. false   2. false   3. true

Big Idea 5: Week 2 • Day 3

A. lenses, eyes
B. 1. B   2. C

Big Idea 5: Week 2 • Day 4

A. Answers will vary—e.g.,
    1. microscope   3. glasses
    2. telescope   4. camera
B. A telescope focuses the sun's rays and makes them stronger when they hit your eye.

Big Idea 5: Week 2 • Day 5

A. 1. bent   2. curved   3. closer
B.

C. 1. lens   2. distorts   3. focus

Big Idea 5: Week 3 • Day 1

A.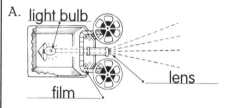

B. 1. false   3. true
    2. true   4. false

Big Idea 5: Week 3 • Day 2

A. 1. light   2. heat
B. 1. The images are hard to see when the lights are on.
    2. The heat from the bulb will melt the film.

Big Idea 5: *Week 3 • Day 3*

A.
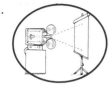

B. Answers will vary—e.g., binoculars, camera
C. A light bulb shines light through the transparency, which is then refracted by a lens.

Big Idea 5: *Week 3 • Day 4*

A. 1. translucent   3. transparent
   2. opaque
B. 2, 1, 4, 3

Big Idea 5: *Week 3 • Day 5*

A. 1. projector   3. focus
   2. film
B.
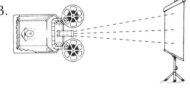
C. The bulbs use less energy because they make less heat.

Big Idea 5: *Week 4 • Day 1*

A.

B. 1. absorbed, reflected
   2. reflected, direction
C. A crinkled piece of foil is not flat or smooth.

Big Idea 5: *Week 4 • Day 2*

A. 1. true   4. false
   2. false   5. true
   3. false
B. Answers will vary—e.g.,
   1. pond   2. tile floor

Big Idea 5: *Week 4 • Day 3*

A. 1. a frozen pond
   2. a marble floor
   3. an empty pool
   4. a silver spoon
B. 1. polish, reflection
   2. transparent, reflection

Big Idea 5: *Week 4 • Day 4*

A. 1. bigger   2. smaller
B. The spoon is curved so the reflected image looks distorted.

Big Idea 5: *Week 4 • Day 5*

A. reflection, reflect, polish
B. Answers will vary.
C. Answers will vary—e.g.,
   1. water   2. windows   3. glasses

Big Idea 5: *Week 5 • Unit Review 1*

1. A   2. C   3. D   4. B   5. A   6. D

Big Idea 5: *Week 5 • Unit Review 2*

Across
1. projector
3. ray
4. absorb
6. radiate
7. opaque
8. focus

Down
2. transparent
3. refract
5. lens
6. reflect

Big Idea 5: *Week 5 • Unit Review 3*

1. Answers will vary—e.g., water in pool, water in glasses, drinking glasses, sunglasses, table
2. Answers will vary—e.g., ground, pool ladder, chairs, blanket, umbrella, woman's hat and bathing suit and sandals
3. Answers will vary—e.g., water in swimming pool, water in glasses, sunglasses
4. Answers will vary—e.g., She is wearing a hat and sunglasses.

Big Idea 5: *Week 5 • Unit Review 4*

1. The objects looked bigger.
2. Light can't pass from air through water in a straight line, so the objects look distorted and larger.
3. The objects would be harder to see because the bag would become less transparent.

Big Idea 6: *Week 1 • Day 1*

A. Answers will vary—e.g.,
   1. lights   2. radio   3. TV
B. 1. false   2. true   3. false
C. 1. 300   2. 60

Big Idea 6: *Week 1 • Day 2*

A. 1. Atoms   3. electrons
   2. protons
B. 1. in the middle of
   2. smaller than

Big Idea 6: *Week 1 • Day 3*

A. positive, negative, negative, positive
B. 1. false   3. true
   2. false   4. true

Big Idea 6: *Week 1 • Day 4*

A. 1. static   2. electrons
B. Answers will vary.

Big Idea 6: *Week 1 • Day 5*

A. static, electrons, protons, charge
B. 1. false   2. true   3. true
C.

Big Idea 6: *Week 2 • Day 1*

A. Answers will vary—e.g.,
   1. radio   3. telephone
   2. computer   4. lamp
B. 1. Electric current
   2. static electricity
   3. electric current
   4. Static electricity

Big Idea 6: *Week 2 • Day 2*

A. 1. false   3. false
   2. true   4. true
B. 1. plug   2. copper   3. conducts

Big Idea 6: *Week 2 • Day 3*

A.

B. Answers will vary—e.g.,
   The thick gloves and boots are insulators that protect people from the electrical current.

Big Idea 6: Week 2 • Day 4

A. 1. true   2. true   3. false
B. salt

Big Idea 6: Week 2 • Day 5

A. appliance, conductor, current, insulator
B. 1. true   2. false   3. true
C. 1. conductor   3. insulator
   2. insulator   4. conductor

Big Idea 6: Week 3 • Day 1

A. 1. circuit
   2. complete
   3. two directions
B. a race track because it forms a continuous loop

Big Idea 6: Week 3 • Day 2

A. 1. false   2. true   3. true
B. Yes, they are using circuits because electricity needs to follow a path.

Big Idea 6: Week 3 • Day 3

A.
B. 1. They always need to be turned on.
   2. No, because the power is still turned on.

Big Idea 6: Week 3 • Day 4

A. electricity, light bulb, heat, light
B. Answers will vary—e.g.,
   Compare: Both make light.
   Contrast: The incandescent bulb has a wire, but the fluorescent bulb does not.

Big Idea 6: Week 3 • Day 5

A.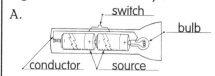

   Captions will vary.
B. 5, 4, 1, 3, 2

Big Idea 6: Week 4 • Day 1

A. 1. true   2. false   3. false
B.

TALK: The smoke detector has a battery that works in case the power goes out.

Big Idea 6: Week 4 • Day 2

A. 1. positive   3. circuit
   2. electricity
B. Answers will vary—e.g.,
   1. video game   3. camera
   2. remote control

Big Idea 6: Week 4 • Day 3

A.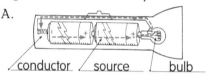
   1. from negative to positive
   2. the battery
B. Answers will vary—e.g., You sometimes need a flashlight outside, so it needs to work without a cord.

Big Idea 6: Week 4 • Day 4

A. 1. false   2. true   3. true
B. Answers will vary—e.g., You use these things a lot.

Big Idea 6: Week 4 • Day 5

A. 1. battery
   2. recharged
   3. positive, negative
B.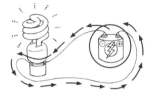

C. 1. false   3. true
   2. false   4. true

Big Idea 6: Week 5 • Unit Review 1

1. C   2. D   3. A   4. B   5. C   6. A

Big Idea 6: Week 5 • Unit Review 2

First paragraph: static, atoms, charges, current, conductors
Second paragraph: sources, batteries, circuit, switch

Big Idea 6: Week 5 • Unit Review 3

3 Wires in the walls carry electricity to the outlets

1 A power plant uses machines to make huge amounts of electrical energy

4 Electricity flows through the insulated cord to the computer

2 Power lines carry electrical energy from the power plant to a house

Big Idea 6: Week 5 • Unit Review 4

1. Answers will vary—e.g., I rubbed it against my sweater.
2. The pull between the atoms on the balloon and the atoms on the can.
3. Answers will vary.